Fifties Flashback

The American Car

Dennis Adler

Dedication

To Jeanne

For looking over my shoulder from time to time and encouraging me every day.

© Dennis Adler, 1996

This edition published in 2012 by
CRESTLINE
a division of BOOK SALES, INC.
276 Fifth Avenue Suite 206
New York, New York 10001
USA

This edition published by arrangement with Motorbooks International, an imprint of MBI Publishing Company.

First published in 1996 by Motorbooks International, an imprint of MBI Publishing Company, 400 First Avenue North, Suite 300, Minneapolis, Minnesota, 55401. Motorbooks International is a certified trademark, registered with the United States Patent Office.

The information in this book is true and complete to the best of our knowledge. All recommendations are made without any guarantee on the part of the author or Publisher, who also disclaim any liability incurred in connection with the use of this data or specific details.

We recognize that some words, model names and designations, for example, mentioned herein are the property of the trademark holder. We use them for identification purposed only. This is not an official publication.

Printed in China
Reprint 2012 (twice), 2013

Library of Congress Cataloging-Publication-Data
Adler, Dennis
    Fifties flashback the American Car / Dennis Adler
        p. cm.
 Includes index.
1.Automobiles—United States. I.Title
TL23.A25 1996
629.222'0973'09045—dc20   96-24919

ISBN-13: 978-0-7858-2831-0

On the front cover: Buick's limited-production 1954 Skylark was number three in GM's Triple Crown—Cadillac Eldorado and Oldsmobile Fiesta being one and two.

On the frontispiece: A Hollywood from the fifties cruises past a Hollywood of the nineties. Hudson, still a strong company in the early fifties, was popular on the streets and successful on the stock car circuit.

On the title page: Cadillac's 1953 Eldorado was one of the most dramatic designs of the early fifties. Built in limited numbers, many of its features would be passed on to production Caddies.

On the back cover:

Top: Perhaps the ultimate expression of the late-fifties automotive aesthetic, the 1959 Cadillac Eldorado. Chrome, towering fins, and more chrome. By the end of the decade, even some of the designers were questioning if things had gone too far.

Bottom: GM's Motorama was an elaborately staged, yearly event to debut new cars as well as the ever-popular "dream cars". *General Motors*

CONTENTS

ACKNOWLEDGMENTS

Sometimes the best place to begin a story is at the end. The year was 1959 and America was ending a decade unlike any other. We had bid farewell to the age of innocence and come through a gauntlet of disparity: The Great Depression in the 1930s, the horrors of World War II, then the "police action" in South Korea, and the rearming of peacetime America in the 1950s.

So much had changed in so short a time that we were spellbound. That sounds laughable by today's standards when changes in world geopolitics and technology are so far-reaching each year, sometimes each month, that the impact of the 1950s amounts to little more than a hiccup in the timeline. In the 1950s, however, every change seemed breathtaking, especially those that took place in the U.S. automobile industry from 1946 to 1959.

Capturing this uniquely American era in pictures and text has been a lengthy endeavor involving several years of photography and research, not only into the automotive industry, but the very heart of the country as it emerged from the postwar 1940s. In preparing this book, I consulted with more than a dozen of the automotive industry's leading designers and reviewed the 1950s in overwhelming detail through the words of author David Halberstam. I probably know more about Nixon, McCarthy, Alger Hiss, Oppenheimer, and the bomb than I will ever need, but the one thing Halberstam so poignantly depicts is the role the automobile had in shaping America throughout the decade. Halberstam's book, *The Fifties,* is a unique chronology of the era, a literary road map that helped guide me through this exciting period.

Outstanding help from people at the Henry Ford Museum, Floyd Joliet from the GM archives, the Indianapolis Motor Speedway Museum, the Chrysler Corporation, and designers David Holls, Charles Jordan, Jack Telnack, Tom Gale, Bill Porter and others require gratitude words alone cannot express. My interviews over the years with such renowned historians and automotive legends as Frank Hershey, Gene Winfield, Zora Arkus-Duntov, Carroll Shelby, Bruce Meyer, Bill Devin, Dean Batchelor, George Walker, Eugene Bordinat, and Alex Tremulis, have provided this book with insights that bring us closer to being there than simple historical narrative can ever hope to.

There are car owners and then there are car collectors. The time invested in restoring a 1955 Ford or a 1959 Cadillac is no less demanding than that required to restore a 1937 Duesenberg. The dedication which each of the following owners has devoted to bring new life to rusted and crumpled metal, torn fabric and frozen engines is deserving of commendation: Lon Berger, 1955 Corvette; Richard Bliss, 1957 Chevrolet; Joe Bortz, 1955 Chrysler Ghia Falcon, 1954 Dodge Firearrow, 1957 Chrysler Diablo; Ron Cressey, 1924 Ford Model Speedster; Jack Denlinger, 1957 Pontiac Bonneville fuelie; Rick Di Cesare, 1957 Ford Retractable; Russell Doane, 1956 Lincoln Continental Mark II; Bob Hardisty, 1957 Lincoln Premiere; Don Hicks, 1959 Chevrolet Impala convertible; Bruce Lustman, "The Outlaw"; John MacArthur, 1956 Packard Caribbean; Chip Miller, 1953 Corvette; Randy Mytar, 1958 Buick Century Caballero Estate Wagon, 1955 Studebaker President; Jerry Palmer, 1953 Hudson Hollywood Hardtop; Petersen Automotive Museum, 1932 Ford hi-boy roadster; Bob Phillips, 1958 Pontiac Bonneville Sport Coupe; Otto Rosenbusch, 1956 Chrysler 300B; Brad Smith, 1947 Ford Super Deluxe; Ron Spindler, 1954 Buick Skylark; Noel Thompson, 1946 Cadillac Series 62 convertible coupe, 1957 Chrysler 300C; Chris Trexler, 1958 Lincoln Continental Mark III; and Jake Williams, 1958 Cadillac Fleetwood Sixty Special.

Others who have contributed to the content of this book include authors T.C. Browne, the late Dean Batchelor, and Bruce Meyer, who provided several of the greatest original hot rods of the 1950s for me to photograph.

There are so many individuals who have in one way or another contributed to this project that it is impossible to mention them all, but in seeing this final work, I hope they will all recognize their contributions and accept my humble thanks.

—Dennis Adler, Imler, Pennsylvania

Three iterations of the original two-seat Thunderbird, 1955, 1956, and 1957. For 1958 the car was completely revamped and expanded to four seats.

PEOPLE, PLACES, AND COUNTLESS THINGS

CHAPTER

Reshaping the Postwar American Landscape

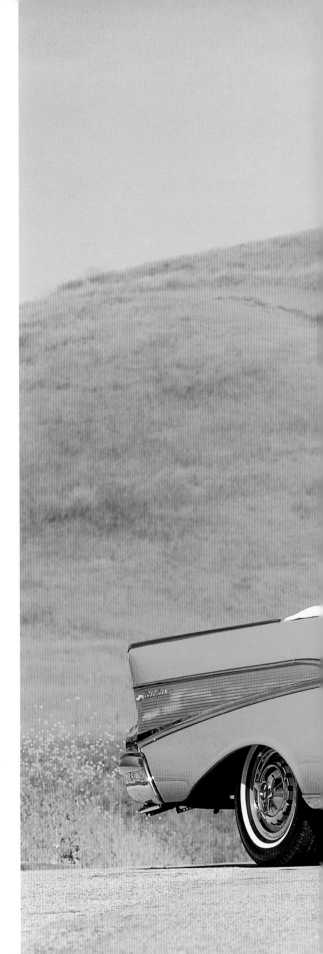

What is it about the past that intrigues us so? Just ahead looms the year 2000, threshold of a new millennium, yet more often than not we find ourselves looking back, rather than ahead—back to a time when Detroit was the center of the world, when automobiles had character, politicians had style and Americans were fascinated by every new gadget that came along.

Consider that our country has little more than two centuries of history and that in this brief period we have gone from flintlock pistols and horse drawn carriages to production automobiles that can reach nearly 200 miles per hour and weapons of such fearsome power that their use has become unconscionable. That which lies ahead, despite all our speculation about the future, is unknown, except for one constant: Mankind's insatiable appetite for change and improvement.

It is change that we address within this book, the history of the automobile in America and how it contributed to reshaping the landscape of this great nation during the 1950s. How can a mere machine have become so important? The answer lies some 90 years in America's past, when five men with a common vision began to change transportation from the horse drawn carriage, and steam locomotive to vehicles powered by the internal combustion engine. Henry Martyn Leland, John and Horace Dodge, Ransom Eli Olds and the architect of modern popular transportation, Henry Ford, were about to alter the course of history.

By 1909 the automobile had already begun to transform our way of life. "Henry Ford put America on wheels," says historian and former General Motors Director of Design Dave Holls. "Instead of spending all your life on the farm you actually got into town and in fact traveled around other states. Everybody loved the automobile in America, and that love affair started with the Model T."

Just as fashion and architecture have followed trends throughout American history, so too have automotive engineering and styling. Unlike fashion, which can change with a whim, or architecture,

Chrome, bumper bombs, and fins defined 1950s automotive styling.

Facelifted and finned from the original trendsetting 1955 Bel Air, Chevrolet's 1957 models would become a quintessential 1950s design.

8

According to Ford Motor Company archives, the last car to roll off an American assembly line before the wartime changeover in 1942 was the Lincoln sedan at right. Ford went from building automobiles to B-24 bombers, produced as quickly and efficiently as cars and trucks. The Ford Motor Company produced 8,685 Liberator bombers at the Willow Run facility. Another plant within the River Rouge complex produced 57,581 Pratt & Whitney R-2800 radial engines. Ford also produced 277,869 standardized military Jeeps. Ford Motor Company

which must endure for decades, even centuries, the automobile evolves in almost perfect 10-year cycles, each clearly mimicking the decade in which it was created. And no decade in American history has been better parodied by the automobile than the 1950s. At the very sight of a Cadillac tailfin one can almost hear Elvis Presley crooning, "Love me tender, love me true," Little Richard screaming "Lucille!," or Milton Berle and Jack Benny bantering in our living rooms courtesy of that wonderful new invention called "television." In 1950, there were already 1.5 million television sets in America. But by 1951 that number would shoot to 15 million!

Aside from the advent of television, no other invention of the 20th century had a greater impact on the way we lived. Although the majority of Americans were not car owners in the 1930s, that quickly changed after the war and so did the role of the automobile in daily life. Roads were improved with the beginning of the U.S. Interstate Highway System, inaugurated in 1956, and by the end of the decade we were not only traveling cross town, across the state, and from coast-to-coast in our cars, we were going to movies and eat-

The majority of early postwar cars were prewar makeovers. One of the first all-new designs was the 1949 Ford. The dramatic new styling gave Ford Motor Company a terrific boost over the crosstown competition at General Motors and Chrysler.
Ford Motor Company

ing breakfast, lunch and dinner in them as well! With the rush to mass personal transit came the drive-in restaurant and drive-in theater. There were even drive-in churches so you could take the family to a Sunday morning sermon and afterwards to the local A&W for a root beer and a burger, delivered right to your car.

The 1950s, as historian and Pulitzer Prize-winning author David Halberstam wrote, was a decade in which Americans exercised personal freedom not in social and political terms, but rather in economic ones. Following financial hardship that had come with the Great Depression and years of sacrifice during World War II, most Americans in the 1950s, Halberstam noted, ". . . needed little coaching in how they wanted to live. They were optimistic about the future. Prices and inflation remained relatively low; and nearly everyone with a decent job could afford to own a home." This was also true of automobile ownership.

Owning a new car and a new home was the American dream. Yes, we were idealistic: Dad went to work, the kids went to school and Mom stayed home, kept house, made dinner and solved all the problems. Or so

we thought. Call it the "Looking for Donna Reed" syndrome. We grew up on it, we believed in it, and perhaps for one brief moment that idyllic way of life even worked. Today, you might call it the Martha Stewart syndrome, only now, Mom can do Dad's job, too.

So much of what Detroit created in the 1950s has become larger than life, although when you consider the height of a 1959 Cadillac tailfin—some 40 inches above the road—maybe it was already larger than life! It is nevertheless The American Way to lionize everything that we remember fondly, especially automobiles. Our cars become historic icons that we mentally click onto in order to recall a time or place. For many, the 1950s represent a piece of Americana most of us can recall either as children or young adults. It was a time when Disneyland was brand new, freeways were rare, shaving cream still came in a tube and highway signs were entertaining.

One of the most successful advertising campaigns in American history was the Burma Shave billboard. Thousands of the dark, painted rectangular signs, always in a series of four, were erected along highways

from coast-to-coast. The Burma Shave rhymes, and there were many different ones, became a part of the American highway landscape. One version that amused children most was the series that read:

"IF YOU WAKE IN HASTE"
"THEN BRUSH YOUR TEETH WITH PASTE"
"AND GET A FUNNY TASTE"
"BURMA SHAVE"

The end of World War II brought a greater prosperity to America than the nation had experienced in years, perhaps greater than at any time in its history. Expectations were high, and the country was ready to embrace change.

"We in this country created the arsenal of democracy with our plants and manufacturing capabilities during the Second World War," explained historian and automotive designer Dave Holls, who joined General Motors in 1952 as a young stylist working under the legendary Harley Earl. "We were able to supply everything the world needed to beat the Axis powers. That was a sensational time when we were all tied together, never as this country had been tied together before. And it was out of this atmosphere of pride and accomplishment that we entered the postwar era."

Early on, Cadillac became Dave Holls' signature car, including the design of that icon of the era, the 1959 Caddy tailfin. "Every science and mechanics magazine in the country [was predicting] the future," remembers Holls. "You've got your new dream home. It's on a semi runway and street, there's a little private helicopter or airplane in the driveway, some are air cars that run on the ground or fly, and that's what people were expecting to see happen someday. In the early postwar era there was nothing that seemed too wild. People weren't afraid of anything and they were waiting for the most breathtaking thing they could

get. It was in this era that the automobile became one of our most important possessions and Detroit became the heart of everything new in this country."

Bill Porter, who has been with GM since 1958, recalls that things were very different in the automobile industry of the 1950s. "In fact," says Porter, "it would be hard to imagine anything more different. We had a tremendously exuberant economy and when I started at GM in the late 1950s, even though it was beginning to wind down a little, you could still feel the excitement in the air. The 1959 Cadillac was already on the boards and every sketch you would do, someone would come along and say, 'Can't you do something newer?' It was always something newer or different, and the guys just exceeded themselves trying to put up the most outrageous things they could think of."

In Detroit, the term "planned obsolescence" was being whispered in board rooms while being served up in wholesale quantities in dealer showrooms. In the 1950s it was typical for new models to offer features that would either be updated or replaced the following model year, and this applied to everything from the engine to the radio. The changeovers were very rapid says Jack Telnack, Ford Motor Company's vice president of Corporate Design. "You look at some of the cars back then, 1957, 1958, 1959, '60, '61, every car was all new sheet metal at Ford, GM and Chrysler. Change was what it was all about in the 1950s and '60s. We thrived on it. When it [yearly changes] stopped, when product cycles became longer, it was because the cost of making changes had increased."

Tom Gale, Vice President Product Design and International Operations for Chrysler, was a design student in the 1950s. Recalls Gale, "When I look back at the fifties I realize that there were some incredible breakthroughs. Virgil Exner's contributions during that era were very significant. I think if you go back and talk to guys like Chuck Jordan, they were dramatically affected by what Exner did. I remember Charlie telling me the story of the time in late 1956 when they hadn't seen the cars and they went down to the lot to look over the fence and see what was going on at Chrysler. They were just blown away by what they saw. Exner had a profound effect on everyone in Detroit."

Chuck Jordan, who retired in 1992 as vice president of Design for General Motors, agrees. "In the fifties, people were anxious, fascinated by what was going to happen in cars. After the war we only had face-lifted models to fill the gap and everybody was waiting for that new generation of cars to come along. However, that really didn't happen in the early fifties, at least not as a great emotional statement, until the 1957 Chryslers came out with the Forward Look and then the 1958 and 1959 cars turned up with all the chrome and fins. It was when we broke out in 1959 that we really let the tiger out of the cage. We did some things that might have been a little overstated, but the right thing to do at the time."

By the early 1950s, the automobile had become the vehicle of choice for family travel. The nation's railroads were in decline and air travel, still relatively new, was prohibitively expensive. Vacationing by car was fast becoming a national passion. The automobile, as Halberstam noted, ". . . was becoming the key to the new tourism." Of course, it had been since the late 1920s, and as more and more Americans took to wandering in the 1930s, highways were marked by tourist cottages, motels and inns, a home away from home for those on the road.

By the early 1950s, an ever increasing number of Americans were making cross-country trips, and it was still in vogue for customers to make the pilgrimage to Detroit by train, take delivery of their new car f.o.b. at the factory, and then drive back home. Along the way, travelers, especially those with small children, were discovering that many of the once cozy, homelike motels scattered along the nation's major highways were turning into ramshackle dumps. One of those travelers was Memphis, Tennessee, home builder Kemmons Wilson, a man who was about to change the face of the American landscape.

Wilson had decided to take his wife and five children to visit the nation's capital, and at the end of each day on the road he was faced with the same search for a motel and a place to eat. After several substandard hotels, it occurred to him that a chain of inns located close to major highways could link cities

together, giving travelers a place to stay where they could expect to find the same quality rooms and a good restaurant at every location. And he could build those hotels the same way he built tract homes. From that simple premise came America's first roadside hotel chain, Holiday Inn.

Spending more and more time in their cars, Americans began to look upon the automobile not only as a means of transportation but also as a source of entertainment. And when it came to being entertained on

As more Americans took to the highways in the 1950s, Memphis, Tennessee, home builder Kemmons Wilson was inspired to create a chain of inns that would offer travelers a place to stay where they could expect consistent quality rooms and a restaurant at every location. Thus was born America's first roadside hotel chain, Holiday Inn.
Holiday Inn

A lot of things were brand new in 1951. Ford offered the Ford-O-Matic automatic transmission for the first time that year. Key starting was also introduced, the key switch now incorporating both the ignition and starter control. The basic bodylines introduced in 1949 were retained, and 1951 models were highlighted by a new dual spinner grille, wraparound bumpers and revised chrome trim.
Ford Motor Company and author

the road nothing was better than tuning in your favorite radio station.

In the 1930s, a car radio was a rare sight and by the 1940s, just as they were becoming popular, World War II intervened. By the 1950s, however, it was almost unthinkable to purchase a new car without one. No matter where you traveled there were AM stations playing music around the clock. What those stations were airing, though, was about to change as drastically as everything else in the 1950s. One day it was Perry Como and Patti Page, the next it was something most people had never heard before, unless they had been exposed to an almost uniquely southern brand of music called rhythm and blues.

Back in 1951 a Cleveland disc jockey named Alan Freed began playing a version of black R&B music called rock 'n' roll. Although back in the early 1950s most radio stations wouldn't play black music, the sound was catching on just the same. Fats Domino was one of the first black singers to make the crossover from R & B to rock 'n' roll, and his brand of music found its way into the heartland of America.

Around the same time, a young entertainer from Macon, Georgia, was redefining the sound of music and has since declared himself the architect of rock 'n' roll. And who can argue? His name was Little Richard and good golly he took the art to a new level and volume!

There were songs written about automobiles as

The General Motors Motorama was one of the year's most eagerly awaited events. The exhibit toured major cities displaying new models and futuristic concept cars. Each GM division had its own advanced styling studio and the Motorama gave designers an opportunity to push the creative envelope, showcasing ideas that might, or might not, appear on future production models. In 1953, GM actually sold several of the concept cars to buyers after the show closed. The following year this practice was discontinued and concept cars were either stored or destroyed after the Motorama. GM archives

far back as the early 1900s, but it was a long road trip from "Come away with me Lucille in My Merry Oldsmobile" to the pounding beat of Jackie Brenston's "Rocket 88," recorded for Sam Phillips in the early 1950s. Phillips said that Brenston's song was a breakthrough recording that really bridged the gap between rhythm and blues and rock 'n' roll. What came next, closed that gap forever.

In June 1953, an 18-year-old truck driver came into Phillips' Memphis studio to record two songs for his mother's birthday. Back then, you could cut your own single for $3.98 at the Memphis Recording Service. Sam Phillips listened as a young singer named Elvis Presley recorded "My Happiness" and "That's When Your Heartaches Begin." Presley was exactly what Phillips had been looking for, hoping for, but had never expected to find—a young white southern boy who could sing rhythm and blues. However, Elvis put his own unique twist on it, what Phillips later described as a mixture of R & B and country.

He put Elvis together with local musicians Scotty Moore and Bill Black to develop songs that would showcase Elvis' distinctive sound. On July 5, 1954, Presley, Moore and Black cut two songs for Phillips' Sun Records label, Bill Monroe's "Blue Moon of Kentucky" and an Arthur "Big Boy" Crudup blues number titled "That's Alright." Three days later, a little over one year from the day Presley first walked into Phillips' studio, Memphis disc jockey Dewey Phillips broke "That's Alright" on his WHBQ "Red Hot, and Blue" radio show. People stared at their radios, and

then they listened and never stopped. Black, white, it didn't matter. Everyone liked it. Elvis Presley marked the dawn of a new era in music. As John Lennon, one of Elvis' admirers, later remarked about the rise of Presley and his importance to the history of rock 'n' roll, "Before Elvis there was nothing."

By the mid 1950s, Elvis, Buddy Holly and the Big Bopper were among legions of new rock 'n' roll singers

filling the airwaves. Artists like Bo Diddley and Chuck Berry were extracting sounds from electric guitars that no one had ever thought possible, or even considered, and a honky-tonk piano man named Jerry Lee Lewis was shakin' up the whole music scene with a frantic style that made Little Richard appear somber. Within a few short years America had a whole new sound coming across the airwaves and drivers were taking to the road tapping out a new beat on the steering wheel that could harmonize with Detroit's hottest V-8s.

There was no question that the automobile had become a national preoccupation, a fact that would not be lost on Detroit. The hierarchy of automobile production was about to launch the greatest changes in manufacturing history—bold, new styling, and advanced engineering techniques that would get into step with the expanding American infrastructure, a proud nation ready to embark on a new decade. Detroit was making certain that wherever Americans were headed, it would be behind the wheel of a new American car.

Chrysler's 1957 models caught GM, Ford, and the rest of the automotive industry by surprise with dramatic new styling developed by design chief Virgil Exner. "He had a profound effect on everyone in Detroit," says Tom Gale, current vice president of Product Design and International Operations for Chrysler.

OPPOSITE
The relationship that grew between Chrysler's chief stylist Virgil Exner and the management of Carrozzeria Ghia in Turin, Italy, brought about some of the most dramatic design concepts of the 1950s. Designed by Exner and built in Italy by Ghia, the 1955 Chrysler Ghia Falcon (silver), 1954 Dodge Firearrow, (yellow), and 1957 Chrysler Diablo (red), all contributed to Dodge, Chrysler, Plymouth, and DeSoto's breakout styling in 1957.

17

RIDING ON THE WINDS OF WAR

CHAPTER 2

The Beginning of the Postwar Era

It would be unfair to jump right into the 1950s without looking back at some of the early postwar models that set the stage for a new era in automotive design.

When World War II came to an end, Americans were frantic for new cars. Nothing had come off a Detroit assembly line in four years that didn't fly, float, ford rivers, or have artillery attached to it somewhere. If you wanted a new car in 1946, you either knew someone in the business or your name ended up at the bottom of a very long waiting list. There were no discounts, and there was no bargaining. The demand for new cars so far outstripped production that the best deal was getting a car at all, and dealers were charging a premium by loading new models with outlandish options.

In a way, this garnishment was fortunate because Detroit had little to offer buyers that wasn't carried over from 1942, not that anyone particularly cared. This was car-starved America, nearly five years without a new model in dealer showrooms and GM found itself in an advantageous position at war's end—their 1942 models had been among the most advanced in styling and engineering.

On October 7, 1945, the first postwar models were announced and Buick was off to a fast start with cars that looked newer than anything else on the market. It was a short-lived launch, however, as the UAW struck General Motors on November 21, which brought production to a grinding halt. The labor relations rhetoric held up the assembly lines for 119 days, but Buick still managed to put 158,728 new cars onto America's highways, moving them into fifth place in total new model sales.

Unlike most automakers that had to face the postwar 1940s with outdated prewar designs, Buick had introduced a new series in 1942 and with just a few changes, such as "Sweeping Airfoil" fenders, models like this Buick Roadmaster looked brand new.

For woodies, a mere wash job was not enough. It was recommended that the cars be treated the same as the planking of a yacht. The wood was to be given a fresh coat of varnish whenever it became dull or weathered. The process was a long and tedious one, which automakers recommended be done every six months to ensure a long-lasting finish and protection from moisture. Models like the 1947 Ford Super Deluxe were all too often neglected over the years and suffered from wood rot long before rust.

a new gun sight hood ornament, another of Nickels' designs that would carry over into the next decade.

By 1947, Buick had taken over the number four sales spot within GM, a position it had held throughout much of the 1930s. Helping regain its sales margin over other GM divisions (except Chevrolet), were two of Buick's most popular models, the Roadmaster and Super convertibles. In 1947 alone, a combined total of 38,371 were sold—nearly 14 percent of Buick's entire production. With 10 different models offered, one out of every seven Buicks sold was a ragtop!

While exterior lines were changed slightly from year to year, mostly by making the grille even larger and more imposing, Buick would hang on to its trump card until the 1948 model year. In January, Buick announced the introduction of the Dynaflow transmission on Roadmaster models. The new shift-free transmission was a crib of Buick's wartime torque-converter-type automatic transmission used in the Hellcat tank destroyer. Earlier automatic gearboxes installed on a few 1938 Buicks (and 1937 Oldsmobile models) had not been overly successful, though Olds and then Cadillac fared well with their Hydra-Matic transmission up through the beginning of the war. Ironically, Buick had developed a far superior design to the Hydra-Matic in the early 1930s called a "Roller" transmission, but production costs resulting in $500 added to the retail price of a Series 90 model killed the project.

The last of Cadillac's prewar styling cues were delivered on the 1946 and 1947 models. The Series 62 was the only convertible model offered.

Both the manual transmission and the Dynaflow carried power from the Buick Series 70 Fireball, valve-in-head, 320.2-cubic-inch straight-eight engine. With Dynaflow, horsepower was raised from 144 to 150 (developed from a 3 7/16x4 5/16 bore and stroke) by increasing the compression ratio from 6.6:1 to 6.9:1.

With the Limited series no longer being produced, the Roadmaster was elevated to the top of Buick's line and came fully equipped with power front windows, adjustable front seat, and new 15-inch Safety-Ride rims with wider cross section 8.20x15-inch four-ply tires.

The cars were built on Buick's low slung X-braced chassis with independent front suspension, live rear axle, coil springs, and four-wheel hydraulic brakes. A new noise-reducing feature was Buick's "Silent-Zone" body mountings and "Vibra-Shield" engine mounts, which absorbed engine vibration through fat rubber pillows around the engine supports. The goal was to isolate driver and passengers from any sense of being in an automobile, and Buick did it better than just about anybody.

Even though Detroit's new cars were only "warmed over" 1942 models, Buick Chief Stylist Ned Nickels (appointed to the top position just in time to rework the first postwar models) was able to create a new look with what Buick called "Sweeping Airfoil" fenders. While Oldsmobile and Pontiac had retained the traditional front fender lines that either ended at or extended part way into the front door panels, Buick carried its all the way back into the rear fenders and skirts—a modernization of the flowing 1920s and 1930s fender lines. It gave the new Buicks a bold, streamlined appearance—one that would be retained well into the 1950s. A broader grille was topped with

Luxury interiors completed the 1948 lineup with finely woven fabrics or optional hand-sewn leather upholstery—it was like driving your living room. Chrome once more played a major design role, accenting virtually every element of the interior from the steering wheel hub to the instrument bezels, the entire center section of the dash, all of the switches, and the push-button radio.

The Series 62 convertible coupes are ranked among the most collectable of all early postwar Cadillac models for their beautiful pontoon fenders, prominent grille and handsome styling.

The 1948 models—the Roadmaster in particular—took Buick around the bend, figuratively speaking, and down a successful road into the 1950s. Buick's gun sight hood ornament had been aimed squarely at the American buyer and sales increases of more than 100 percent between 1948 and 1950 proved they were right on target.

Cadillac was particularly well positioned for the postwar resumption of car manufacturing. GM Design Chief Harley Earl and Cadillac Design Studio Head Bill Mitchell had made significant styling changes for 1942, the marque's 40th anniversary. Such fortuitous timing gave the GM luxury division a leg up when automobile production resumed after the war. Switching the assembly lines from M-24 Chaffee light tanks to sedans and convertibles was no mean feat, yet it took Cadillac only two months, from August 15 to early October, by which time gasoline rationing had officially ended and the War Production Board had lifted all restrictions on civilian passenger car production.

As with other GM divisions, designs at Cadillac varied little from 1942. Revised styling for 1946 featured a new grille with six large horizontal bars and new three-piece front and rear bumpers. The most significant restyling was the Cadillac emblem, which was changed to a majestic gold V surrounding a Cadillac crest.

In 1946, Cadillac promoted its V-8 engines as "battle-proven" because every new car had a 346-cubic-inch V-8 which could be backed up by an optional Hydra-Matic transmission, similar to those used to power the 12,000 Cadillac-built M-5, M-8, M-19 and M-24 tanks. (To the chagrin of those who purchased war-surplus Cadillac tank engines and Hydra-Matic transmissions, they were not suitable for automotive use. Cadillac's Clark Street headquarters actually had to issue a dealer bulletin warning that the use of surplus engines and transmissions ". . . should not be encouraged." The bulletin related the plight of one Cadillac owner who installed an M-24 tank engine and transmission in his prewar car only to find that it had three reverse speeds and one forward speed! Not surprising since the tank engines ran in reverse.)

Cadillac's first postwar models were coupes and sedans, with nearly half of the year's production of 29,194 cars consisting of Series 62 four-door sedans. The stylish Series 62 convertible coupe didn't make its appearance until late in the model year and then only 1,342 came off the assembly line.

The 1946 and 1947 Series 62 convertible coupes are ranked among the most collectable of all early postwar Cadillac models for their beautiful pontoon fenders, prominent grille, and handsome styling. The Series 62 was the only convertible model offered, and the 1946 and 1947 models were the most attractive Cadillacs of the 1940s.

How great was the demand for new Cadillacs? The GM division closed the books on 1947 production in mid January 1948 with more than 96,000 unfilled orders!

Detroit automakers all faced the same problem after the war: how to produce new cars from prewar tooling. One very clever solution used by both Ford and Chrysler was to capitalize on an even older idea: the plywood-paneled station wagon.

Wood panels had been used on station wagons by Detroit automakers (and others) as far back as the 1920s, and wood planking as an exterior design element had been used by coachbuilders in the early 1900s, particularly in France. Faced with the need to distinguish postwar models that had little or no sheetmetal differences from their prewar brethren, both Ford and Chrysler decided to produce sedans and convertibles accented with wood body paneling rather than limiting the distinctive application solely to station wagons.

Ford had been the first of Detroit's Big Three to go into production with a wood-bodied wagon, introducing its new models in 1945, only three months after the war had ended. Ford and Mercury once again shared body styles, basically unchanged from 1942. The most significant difference was redesigned grillework on both the Deluxe and Super Deluxe bodies. Red striping detail in the grille on '46 Fords set them apart from the later 1947–48 models. There were also a number of minor changes used by Ford to distinguish model years, such as parking lamp designs and hood ornaments. After the first full year of postwar production, Ford was ready to expand its line of wood

Leather trim and Hydro-Lectric power windows were standard on Cadillac's Series 62 convertible coupe.

During this same period, Ford jumped on the bandwagon with the Sportsman Convertible. The car was Henry Ford II's idea, based on a concept penned by Ford Styling Director Bob Gregorie, who had built a Model A convertible on this order just as the war ended.

Manufacturing the Sportsman, or any of the early postwar woodies for that matter, entailed more than just having wood pieces cut to fit standard production bodies. At Ford, the two-door ragtops had to have special rear body panels made up from 1941 sedan delivery fenders. The taillights were also of 1941 vintage—no doubt making this an interesting car to restore almost 50 years later. The Sportsman Convertibles were continued through 1948 with total production of 3,487.

The majority of wood-panel bodies were not built by the automakers themselves, but were supplied by firms such as J. T. Cantrell, Mid-State Body, U.S. Body and Forging, Hercules, Pekin Wood Products, and Ypsilanti Furniture. The one exception was Ford Motor Company, which owned a timber mill in Iron Mountain, Michigan, and manufactured its own coachwork for the Ford and Mercury station wagons and stylish Ford and Mercury Sportsman convertibles.

General Motors had most of their coachwork done outside, chiefly by Ypsilanti, makers of the Ionia body, and by Hercules. The J. T. Cantrell and Son Company of Huntington, Long Island, also produced several stunning custom Estate Wagons for Cadillac in 1941, and GM's Fisher Body Division had a brief tenure assembling Chevrolet, Oldsmobile and Pontiac station wagons.

Pekin Wood Products, a subsidiary of Chrysler Corporation, produced the white ash and mahogany panels for Chrysler's Town & Country line. Pekin built the wood components, Briggs coachworks assembled the steel body parts, and the cars were completed at Chrysler's Jefferson Avenue plant in Detroit.

The workmanship and time that went into the assembly of these automobiles truly defied reason. The retail price of Ford and Chrysler sedans, convertibles and wagons was significantly greater than similar steel-bodied models. They were also more expensive to repair and equally perplexing to maintain. The notion of calling them land yachts was less of a compliment than it was a forewarning about the care these cars would demand from their owners. By 1950, it was already apparent that wood was no longer the novelty it had been in 1945.

In the early postwar years, wood had given old models a fresh look and provided American automakers with the respite they needed to design and build completely new cars. With that accomplished, the time had come for the woodie to gracefully bow out of the picture.

While America's Big Three were planning their futures, independents like newly formed Kaiser-Frazer and one of the country's oldest established

In 1948, Harley Earl and the GM design staff gave Cadillac a new look with the introduction of tailfins. The original Cadillac tailfin was one of Earl's most dramatic and trendsetting designs. Fascinated with aircraft throughout his career, Earl's inspiration for the 1948 tailfin was the dramatically profiled twin boom rudders on Lockheed's P-38 Lightning fighter plane.

Adding wood to sedan and convertible models gave Chrysler a fresh look for the early postwar era. Ford followed suit with the Sportsman convertible. Chrysler Corporation

paneled models to include a new convertible. Chrysler, however, beat Ford out of the gate.

In 1946, Chrysler introduced the Town & Country convertible built atop the C-39 Series 127.5-inch-wheelbase chassis, and powered by the 135-horsepower flat-head Spitfire Eight. In addition there was a companion four-door sedan, mounted on the C-38 Series 121.5-inch platform and equipped with the 114-horsepower L-head six. Chrysler also offered a one-year-only production run of 100 C-39 Spitfire Eight sedans in 1946, produced on the longer 127.5-inch chassis. With a base price of $2,718 it was some $350 more than the C-38 sedan.

The Town & Country four-door sedan and two-door convertible proved to be relatively popular models. From 1946 to 1948, a total of 3,994 sedans were produced and 8,368 convertibles. In 1949, the Town & Country was restyled and offered in two versions, station wagon and two-door convertible. This would be the final year for the convertible and in 1950 the Town & Country would fade from the scene altogether with two final models, the Newport hardtop sedan, limited to only 698 units, and a 6-passenger Royal station wagon.

"The front looked like town, the back looked like country," someone once said. Either way, in 1946, 1947, and 1948, Chrysler Town & Country models looked great.

Following Chrysler's introduction of the Town & Country convertible, Ford introduced the Ford and Mercury Sportsman convertibles which were based on a concept by Bob Gregorie, Ford's styling director. Gregorie had designed and built a Model A convertible on this order just as World War II ended. One could assume that both Ford and Chrysler struck on the same idea for creating a freshened and uniquely styled early postwar model. Unlike Chrysler and General Motors, which had wood bodies for station wagons, sedans, and convertibles produced by outside contractors or subsidiaries, Ford manufactured its own coachwork for its station wagons and Sportsman convertibles.
Automobile Quarterly

automakers, Studebaker, were both out of the blocks with brand new models by 1947. Studebaker's designs by international stylists Raymond Loewy and Virgil Exner shocked everyone, in or out of the industry.

Studebaker had the longest history of any American automaker, and a heritage dating back to 1852 when the South Bend factory started building wagons. In 1897, Studebaker was one of the first American companies to experiment with an electric carriage, and two years later it began building bodies for electric cars. South Bend's first gasoline-engined car was produced in 1904 using a General Automobile Company of Cleveland, 16-horsepower, two-cylinder chassis.

By the 1920s, Studebaker was one of the most successful automakers in North America with seven factories, four in South Bend, two in Detroit, and one in Ontario, Canada.

Financially, Studebaker suffered badly through the Great Depression, finally going into receivership in 1933. The company was saved by Harold Vance and Paul Hoffman, who had been vice-presidents of sales and engineering, respectively. They raised $1 million in 1935 by auctioning off the assets of the luxurious Pierce-Arrow division which Studebaker

had only acquired in 1928. By 1935, sales had picked up and Vance and Hoffman had Studebaker out of the red, just as America began its climb out of the Depression.

Increased sales added to Studebaker's prosperity up to the beginning of World War II. Substantial military contracts for 6x4 and 6x6 trucks, the amphibious Weasel, and the manufacture of Wright Cyclone aero engines sustained the South Bend firm throughout the conflict. Studebaker emerged from the war in very healthy financial shape, but after a great start in the postwar era, sales began to decline as the new car boom evaporated and Detroit became more competitive. By the early 1950s, Studebaker's fortunes began to fade.

Then there was Preston Thomas Tucker, who tried and failed to do what many had tried and failed to do before him.

The late Alex Tremulis was the Tucker Torpedo's designer. Tremulis believed that Preston Tucker had a car that could have rivaled Detroit's best had outside intervention not foiled his plans.

Early in 1946, Tucker set up the Tucker Corporation in Chicago and announced his intention to introduce an entirely new kind of automobile, one that featured a water-cooled, rear-mounted engine and a lengthy list of safety features. Preston Tucker billed his project as "the first really new car in 50 years."

At one time, Tucker had worked for race car designer Harry Miller, so he was well educated in both the engineering and production sides of the business. The innovative Torpedo was to be a rear-engined sedan with automatic transmission, disc brakes, independent suspension, padded dashboard, and a safety pop-out windshield. The body design by Tremulis was as advanced in its composition as Tucker's mechanical and engineering design. Plagued with setbacks and a need to raise additional capital, Tucker altered his original design in order to get cars into production, but in mid-1948, after seeking an additional $30 million from the federal government's Reconstruction Finance Committee, the watchdog Securities and Exchange Commission determined that in building a

Packard had redesigned its Clipper models for 1942 and had barely put the new cars into production when World War II started. The styling was grand for 1942 but when postwar production picked up, the Clipper looked dated. The company rushed to create an entirely new look for 1948 and in so doing produced a car that was awkward in proportions and less than revered by the automotive press which lampooned the new models with nicknames like "goat" and "bathtub." Packard never recovered, and new styling in the 1950s failed to recapture the once great luxury marque's market share. Packard would not survive the decade.

Preston Thomas Tucker tried and failed to do what many had tried and failed to do before him, namely take on the Detroit establishment. Tucker's plans to build the first really new car in 50 years, with a water-cooled, rear-mounted engine and a lengthy list of safety features, died after only 51 cars were produced. Tucker stylist Alex Tremulis once remarked that the Tucker had a lot of good features but Preston Tucker had too many enemies in Detroit to succeed.
Automobile Quarterly

The 1942 Packard Clipper was a benchmark design, principally created for Packard by Howard "Dutch" Darrin. The design was reprised in 1946 and 1947, but appeared too dated for the postwar era. The all-new 1948 models were based on the 1942 Clipper's lines, which suffered badly in the remake.

car that was materially different from his original prospectus, Tucker had defrauded the government and his investors. To this day, there are still those who believe that the Detroit establishment was behind the Securities and Exchange Commission investigation and Tucker's subsequent indictment.

By the time Tucker was able to clear himself and his company of any wrongdoing, too much time had been lost and what could have been one of the most advanced cars of the postwar era became one of its most eminent failures. Only 51 cars were produced before Tucker was forced into liquidation. Today, Tuckers are considered highly collectable and the remaining examples are valued at over $250,000 each.

The majority of independent automakers such as Studebaker, Packard, Hudson, Kaiser-Frazer, Crosley, and Nash all began the postwar era with consumer demands that far outstripped their production capabilities. But as the new-car pipeline began to fill and the need arose to design and produce new models at the same pace as General Motors, Ford and Chrysler, their futures began to dim, and by the late 1950s nearly all had been forced out of business.

A DECADE TO REMEMBER

CHAPTER 3

When Detroit Was the Center of the World

There is an almost charismatic allure to Detroit's "Big Steel" cars—dazzling, chrome-laden automobiles, built by men, spending their shifts in monotonous, repetitious toil on a never-ending stream of cars. It was a period in this country when foreign makes were little more than that— *foreign*—and the American car ruled the roads.

As the United States entered the 1950s, Detroit's automotive hierarchy was pondering what it was that Americans wanted most in a new car. It came down to three essentials: styling, ease of operation, and performance, in that order.

At General Motors, Harley Earl directed the restyling of all five divisions in the early 1950s and ordered his staff to create a new shape, featuring a low, wide, flat hood in front, with matching decklid in the rear. Recalls Chuck Jordan, "Harley Earl had very specific opinions about design. He used to say, 'My sense of proportion tells me that oblongs are more attractive than squares, just as a ranch house is more attractive than a square three-story flat-roofed house or a greyhound is more attractive than a bulldog.'" Jordan said, "[Earl's] formula was simple enough, 'design cars that are longer, lower, wider.'" These guidelines applied to virtually every GM model being designed, each car sharing a roofline, window shape, and doors that dipped stylishly down into the rear fenders.

The budgetary demands of producing cars for five different divisions posed a problem for GM designers—how to come up with Oldsmobile, Buick, Cadillac, Pontiac and Chevrolet models that wouldn't all look alike. Ford and Chrysler had fewer model lines, so this was not nearly as great a

The 1958 Continental Mk III's unusual canted headlamps and heavy proportions were not popular. Lincoln swept it under the rug with such total disregard that in 1968 the Mk III name was used again on another Continental model.

The Big Steel era was born in 1953 when Cadillac introduced the limited edition Eldorado. Built for only one year, total production of these benchmark cars was just 532. More than just a sportier model, it was a trendsetting design, introducing such innovations as the Panoramic wraparound windshield, cut-down doors (reprising the rakish look of the classic Darrin Packard), and a flush-fitting metal boot that completely concealed the Orlon acrylic fabric convertible top when it was lowered.

GM's Pontiac Division offered a sportier, more prestigious line of cars by the mid-1950s, and with Chevrolet, provided General Motor's strongest appeal to youthful buyers. Models like the Tri-Power-equipped Bonneville were high-performance models targeted at the same market as Chrysler's 300 Series. Models like the 1958 Bonneville were accented by a new chromed side treatment featuring spear-shaped side moldings with a "projectile motif," and sculptured rear quarter panel with four Pontiac stars.

problem. Independents like Hudson, Nash, Packard, and Studebaker had the ability to design new cars with fewer manufacturing limitations than Detroit's big guns, since they had fewer model lines. The problem was that once new models were introduced modest companies like Kaiser-Frazer could not afford to make significant styling changes. Failing to keep pace with competition from GM, Ford and Chrysler led most of the independent automakers to ruin by the end of the decade.

Within GM's structuring of divisions, three bodies, the A, B, and C, were divided among Buick, Oldsmobile, Pontiac, Chevrolet and Cadillac. Buick and Olds shared the B, while Cadillac based its cars on the C, with Pontiac and Chevrolet building cars on the A platform. There were exceptions to the rule, how-

ever, including the Buick Roadmaster, which was built on the larger Cadillac chassis.

All three basic bodies were conceived simultaneously but introduced over a two-year period, with Buick, Olds, and Cadillac in 1954, followed by Pontiac and Chevrolet in 1955.

The 1955 Pontiacs were the division's first entirely new postwar models. Making a clean break with late-1940s styling, they incorporated more changes than any new model since the marque's introduction in 1926. No fewer than 109 new features were included in the 1955 model line.

All new GM models had Panoramic windshields and wraparound backlights, thin front and rear win-

dow posts and the cut-down doors first seen at the 1953 GM Motorama on the Cadillac Eldorado, Oldsmobile Fiesta, and Buick Skylark. Distinction among GM models was achieved through individual radiator grille designs, chrome trim, headlight shapes, lower quarter panel treatments, and taillight details. The 1955 and 1956 Pontiacs, for example, were differentiated from other GM models by a variety of styling cues. Up front, the bumpers had bright, massive dual impact bars and a connecting grille bar, although there was no actual grille behind it. Instead, Pontiac drew upon one of Harley Earl's favorite themes: aircraft styling. A jet-like air intake took the place of the traditional grille opening.

Among Pontiac's most memorable and distinctive styling cues were the fanjet-type crescents above the headlamps, and the broad dual silver hood streaks which started at the grille arch and carried back over the hood to the cowl. Chrome trimmed the bottom of the rear fenders, and optional brightwork skirts added another accent to the rear wheel openings. Overall, the new Pontiac line, the Star Chief in particular, had achieved Earl's objective: shedding the bulky look of the 1940s.

Back in 1955, automotive magazines pegged the Chevrolet Bel Air as the model most likely to be sought-after and predicted that 1955 would be a benchmark year for the company. After all, it was the first time since 1920 that GM's low-priced leader would be powered by a V-8. Challenging the industry-leading Ford V-8 for the first time ever, the Chevrolet's revolutionary new engine would become the springboard for a new generation of automotive enthusiasts.

Designed by Chevrolet Chief Engineer Ed Cole, the new 90-degree Turbo-Fire V-8 had a bore and stroke of 3 3/4x3 inches, and displaced 265 cubic inches. Output for the engine ranged from 162 horsepower at 4,400 rpm, up to 180 horsepower at 4,600 rpm when equipped with the "power-pack" option of four-barrel carbs, special air cleaner, special intake manifold, and dual exhausts. This top option was the most powerful engine Chevrolet had ever offered and public response to the new V-8 was immediate and overwhelming.

In addition to boosting Chevy's performance on the showroom floor, the V-8 version helped polish the division's motorsports image, racking up a total of 13 wins in 25 NASCAR short track events and virtually dominating NHRA racing throughout the 1955 season. And if that wasn't enough to get the public's attention, a white and red Bel Air convertible was selected as the Pace Car for the 39th Indianapolis 500 Mile Race. Chevrolet upped the performance ante even further after Indy by offering the Corvette's 195-horsepower V-8 as an option on any model.

Chevrolet produced a record 2,223,000 cars and trucks in 1955—accounting for nearly one-quarter of all U.S. auto and truck sales!

Aside from the V-8's notoriety, Chevy's seemingly overnight success could be attributed, for the most part, to a shift in image. The change in styling from 1954 to 1955 was in full measure. There was virtually nothing to speak of—save the name and the bow tie emblem—associating the two model years. Chevrolet had gone from producing a dowdy family car to building a young man's car with sportier, more distinctive styling. A car that was right in tune with the 1950s. *Time* magazine

When "Bunkie" Knudsen took over as Pontiac General Manager in June 1956, he believed that horsepower and performance would be the key to Pontiac's future success. The 1957 Bonneville was Knudsen's first step. Initially, the Bonneville was a limited-production model available only as a convertible, and powered by a new 370-cubic-inch fuel-injected V-8, developing 310 horsepower. A stock Bonneville fuelie could romp from 0 to 60 miles per hour in 8.1 seconds and power through the quarter mile in 18 seconds flat.

One of the few mainstream Big Steel cars, the 1957 Buick Century Riviera was called the "banker's hotrod" for its powerful engine and agile performance. Of all the Buicks available in 1957, the Riviera was the fastest. It had the big, 364-cubic-inch, 300-horsepower, V-8 engine, the same one used in the Roadmaster, but the Century models were built on a shorter and lighter 122-inch wheelbase.

In 1953, Americans got a look at something completely different from any automobile they had ever seen, at least from a Detroit automaker. It was the Chevrolet Corvette, a two-passenger sports car with a body manufactured out of plastic. The innovative new model was a sensation at the GM Motorama, one of four "Dream Cars" shown for 1953. Demand was so high that Chevrolet put the Corvette into immediate production. It had originally been planned as a 1954 model, but Chevrolet managed to build 300 cars for 1953.

In 1955 years later, the all-new V-8-powered Chevrolet Bel Air led the starting grid around the Brickyard and a new generation of buyers into Chevy showrooms. Author collection

described it as having "All the anxious looks a young father-to-be bestows on his wife."

The pendulum swing in styling, from conservative to unabashed, brought with it design elements that had previously eluded Chevrolet, and for the most part, all of General Motors. The look of the 1940s and all the vestigial traces of the late 1930s had finally been put to rest by Harley Earl. His revolutionary new styling for 1955 opened the door on a new era for Chevrolet and the American automobile.

The 1955 Chevy's wide grille opening, which observers were quick to note resembled the front of a Ferrari sports car—a connection Harley Earl readily acknowledged—highlighted a list of styling cues that endowed every model from sporty two-door hardtops and convertibles to station wagons, with a unique appearance.

The 1955 Chevys were the first automobiles in the low-price field to reflect the "dream car" influence of the General Motors Motoramas. All of the roof lines had been lowered with a corresponding reduction in hood and belt lines to accent the longer, sportier styling and new wrap-around windshield design. Built on the same 115-inch wheelbase as the 1949 through 1954 models, the new Chevys were one inch shorter in overall length at 195.6 inches.

One of several design innovations introduced in 1955 was the greater use of glass in structural areas, such as the rear quarters. Curved glass actually had greater structural rigidity than sheet metal, allowing Chevy designers to significantly narrow the rear or "C" pillars which were now accented by windows rather than sheet metal. This modification improved both the appearance of the car and the driver's over-the-shoulder visibility.

Beneath the stylish bodywork, the 1955 Chevrolets featured a new frame with stiffer side members engineered to reduce chassis flexing and a new four-point engine mounting system designed to reduce vibration. At the front, a modern version of the ball joint suspension enhanced cornering ability and steering response while Chevy's new control arm geometry canceled out front-end dive induced by hard braking. At the rear, leaf springs were increased 9 inches to an overall length of 58 inches and the mounts were relocated outside of the frame in a fashion similar to that used on the Corvette. The result was a more comfortable "luxury car ride" without the sacrifice of handling.

From behind the wheel, Chevy owners were treated to a new sense of performance and responsiveness with a revised Powerglide automatic trans-

mission designed to deliver quicker acceleration and throttle response.

The interior of 1955 models took on a look as sporty as the exterior with a dash and instrument layout lifted from the Corvette but accented with a wide band of chrome mesh. Seats were deep, soft, and comfortable, and upholstery fabrics in the more expensive Bel Air models were top quality woolens, nylons, and leatherettes.

Summed up, the 1955 Chevrolet line—from the base six-cylinder 150 Series to the top-of-the-line V-8-powered Bel Air models—was a gathering together of the best mechanical and design features Detroit had to offer. In one year, Chevrolet redefined itself, becoming the most popular car in America.

At the other end of the spectrum was the most luxurious car in America, the Cadillac. GM's luxury car division literally created the "Big Steel" era back in 1953 with a single model: the Eldorado. It was probably the most publicized debut of a new car in history. The very first Eldorado built was given to President Dwight David Eisenhower by General Motors for use in his inaugural parade. A classic 1950s press photograph shows Ike standing in the back of the Eldorado, arms outstretched in triumph.

The 1953 Eldorado was a one-year-only model. That may sound contradictory, since the Eldorado is still produced today, but the original version was a special edition limited to only 532 examples. The following year the Eldorado became little more than a tarted up version of the Series 62 convertible, priced $2,000 less than in 1953 and built in such numbers as the market would absorb.

As the first of the Big Steel cars, the 1953 Eldorado established a niche which lasted throughout the decade, culminating with the most overstated convertible Cadillac of all time, the 1959 Eldorado Biarritz. However, the last word on the subject of excess belongs to the Cadillac Fleetwood Sixty Special.

The Sixty Special was the epitome of Cadillac's big road car image, one of the largest automobiles produced during the 1950s. Although Cadillac may have only sold a thousand a month nationwide, the Sixty Special always attracted showroom traffic, and for every one that failed to find a buyer, someone, somewhere was inspired to make a down payment on the more affordable Series Sixty Two.

When the Ford design staff decided to "out-chrome and out-fin" Cadillac, they penned the biggest Lincolns and Continentals ever produced—wider, longer, lower, more powerful, more luxurious, and heavier than any before.

Lincoln's early postwar efforts were upstaged by Cadillac, even Oldsmobile. The new postwar Lincolns, despite their improved suspensions, better brakes, stronger frames, and more powerful engines were not perceived by the public as being equals to Cadillac.

In the early 1950s, the Lincoln Division turned its attention toward high performance, establishing an enviable reputation in a new arena: motorsports competition. For four consecutive years—1952 through 1955—Lincoln dominated the Carrera Panamericana road races in Mexico. Unfortunately, Lincoln's new performance image did little in the quest for sales over Cadillac. In fact, it had quite the opposite effect. It appeared to some consumers as though Lincoln had

abandoned the luxury field to Cadillac altogether. Between 1947 and 1955, Cadillac sales increased by two and a half times, while Lincoln's volume rose by only 42 percent. In spite of these less than inspiring numbers, Lincoln produced an excellent automobile that offered race-proven engineering and performance at a reasonable price.

So in 1956, Lincoln decided to go bumper-to-bumper with GM's luxury division. The new generation Lincoln was seven inches longer and 100 pounds heavier than the 1955 models, and fully eight inches longer than a 1956 Cadillac Series Sixty Two! Under the hood was a powerful 368-cubic-inch V-8 that endowed the cars with chest-swelling acceleration and top speed.

The completely restyled 1956 models were honored with the Industrial Design Institute's award for excellence in automotive design. Lincoln finally had a winner. Sales for the model year rose to 50,322, exclusive of the Continental Mark II, which was classed as a separate line. It became Lincoln's best year since 1949.

As a result of this achievement, Lincoln was finally in a position to take on Cadillac, and could have, had they left well enough alone. In 1958, Lincoln introduced another all-new model line, one that would draw more attention for its avant garde styling than it would buyers with cash in hand. The 1958 Lincolns presented a radical departure from the past. Now of unibody construction—the largest unibody cars of their time—they were built side-by-side with the new four-passenger Thunderbirds. However, all of the weight saving gains associated with the new construction process (which did away with the traditional separate chassis) were lost in the sheet metal added to keep the massive cars from buckling under their own weight. As a result the new models weighed a minimum of 4,735 pounds, several hundred more than the cars they replaced.

The new Lincolns stretched over 19 feet and appeared even larger. At the front, canted quad headlamps gave the cars a striking, albeit odd, appearance, and deeply sculpted front fenders made the body look even more massive. The total effect was appalling. Aside from the Edsel, this would be Ford Motor Company's biggest disappointment of the 1950s. The prestige Lincoln Division had taken sharp aim at Cadillac and shot itself in the foot.

Lincoln's woes in the 1950s, however, paled next to the difficulties experienced by another prestigious American nameplate, Packard. One of America's oldest automotive names (founded in 1899), Packard had declined from an industry Brahmin in the 1930s to a financially troubled shadow of its former self by the early 1950s. Packard's early postwar efforts were too closely tied to prewar designs and by the time models like the sporty Caribbean were introduced, the company was in serious trouble. By 1954, sales had plummeted to only 27,307 cars. Packard was on its deathbed and corporation CEO James Nance, was holding the smoking gun.

William C. Durant had created General Motors by bringing independent automakers together under a single banner. Nance and George Mason, head man at Nash-Kelvinator in Kenosha, Wisconsin, were about to attempt the same thing in 1954 by merging Packard with Studebaker and Nash with Hudson. The joint mergers would give Mason's American Motors a complete line of cars from trend-setting compacts to full-size luxury cars plus the prestige of the Hudson and Packard passenger cars and Studebaker's popular line of trucks.

Mason completed the merger with Hudson on April 22, 1954. Nance compelled Packard's board of directors to merge with Studebaker in October. As it turned out, Studebaker was in far worse financial shape than Nance had expected and the merger with Mason's new American Motors Corporation was the only way to save Studebaker-Packard. It was not to be. On October 8, 1954, George Mason died, taking with

him the only power that could have bound both companies. His successor at AMC, George Romney, decided it would be in the company's best interest not to merge with the financially ailing Studebaker-Packard. Nance was lost and so was Packard, which was ultimately scraped in order to save Studebaker. The last Packards were merely rebadged Studebakers, and in 1958 the name was dropped altogether. Packard was no more and America had lost one of its greatest automotive namesakes.

Chrysler waded through the 1950s with a wide variety of models, perhaps the most famous of which was the 300 Series. It was everything an automotive enthusiast could ask for in a family car.

The original Chrysler 300 was the first production model to deliver a wheel-spinning 300 horsepower when the hammer was dropped. With a 331-cubic-inch V-8 stuffed under the hood, the 1955 models were flat out hell on wheels. The stock V-8s were equipped with two Carter four-barrel carburetors and a solid lifter camshaft of the same grind American sportsman Briggs Cunningham used in his 1954 Chrysler Le Mans racing engines. These changes boosted horsepower from 250 to the magic 300.

In 1956, the Chrysler 300B became the American stock car racing champion, racking up 37 AAA and NASCAR titles, and an Unlimited Stock Class victory at Daytona. The 300C continued the tradition at Daytona in 1957, becoming the fastest stock sedan in the world.

Back in the mid-1950s, all of this performance was packaged rather sedately. *Mechanix Illustrated*'s automotive editor, Tom McCahill, aptly described the

After long negotiations, Studebaker-Packard was purchased by the Curtiss Wright aircraft company in 1956. The significant infusion of cash from Curtiss-Wright, along with new defense contracts and the North American distribution rights for Mercedes-Benz vehicles, put Studebaker-Packard on the road to recovery. However for Packard, the consolidation led to an in-name-only line of modestly restyled Studebakers bearing the Packard name. The most notorious badge-engineered South Bend, Indiana, model was the Packard Hawk, based on the 1957 Studebaker Golden Hawk. Automobile Quarterly

300 series as "...competition cars in a full Brooks Brothers suit...." As image builders, these cars were omnipotent at Daytona and in motorsports competition across America, but when it came to turning heads at a stop light, they DNF'd.

Chrysler, despite building a quality product, was burdened with a stodgy, old-man's-car image that designer Virgil Exner was convinced he could change. A conceptualist known for the character of his designs, Exner was shrewd enough to know he would need outside help to reverse the tide at Chrysler. He turned to Mario Boano and the Carrozzeria Ghia in Turin, Italy, to develop his Idea Cars, designs that Exner believed would propel Chrysler a generation ahead of Ford and GM styling. His "Forward Look" put Chrysler at the forefront of American automobile style, a direct result of the Chrysler-Ghia relationship that began in 1951.

The dynamics of new model styling in the early 1950s was exemplified by the cars chosen to pace the annual Indianapolis 500. In 1951 it was a Chrysler convertible with smart but contemporary styling.

Chrysler was one of the first automakers to venture into the high-performance field. While many auto enthusiasts consider the late 1960s as the birth of the muscle car, the original Chrysler 300 certainly qualifies as the mother of all muscle cars. It was the first production car to deliver a wheel-spinning 300 horsepower when the hammer was dropped. In 1956, the Chrysler 300B became the champion of American stock car racing, racking up 37 AAA and NASCAR titles, and an Unlimited Stock Class victory at Daytona.

OPPOSITE
The 1958 Cadillac Fleetwood Sixty Special was the epitome of "Big Steel" era cars. The Sixty Special weighed almost two tons and when equipped with the rear-mounted spare was nearly 19-feet long. In 1958, this was one of the largest cars on American roads. It was also one of the least produced models in the Cadillac line. Only 12,900 were built for the entire year, and of that, only a fraction were ordered with the optional factory Continental spare.

In the early 1950s, Virgil Exner turned to Mario Boano and the Carrozzeria Ghia in Turin, Italy, to help in developing new designs that Exner believed would propel Chrysler a generation ahead of Ford and GM styling. The most dramatic result of Exner's Ghia concept cars came in 1957 with the totally redesigned 300C, distinguished from all other 1957 models by a massive grille based on an inverted rendition of the 1955 Ghia Falcon grille. The new edifice would become a Letter Car trademark through 1959, and influence Chrysler styling well into the 1960s.

By taking advantage of low construction costs in Italy, along with the coachwork's fine craftsmanship, Exner and Ghia produced some of the most beautiful concept cars ever to flow from a designer's pen—the d'Elegance and Chrysler Specials, the DeSoto Adventurer II, Dodge Firearrow and Chrysler Falcon, to name but a few.

The transatlantic relationship between Chrysler and Ghia also brought forth a series of limited production models beginning in 1953 with the Chrysler Ghia GS-1 coupes, a series of 400 cars closely resembling Exner's 1952 Chrysler Special and sold exclusively in Europe by Societe France Motors. The limited production 1954 Dodge Firebomb cabriolet and the Chrysler-powered Dual Ghias were sold by Detroit-based Dual Motors from 1956 to 1958. Dual Ghia became *the* car for Hollywood celebrities, including Frank Sinatra, Peter Lawford, Dean Martin, and Sammy Davis, Jr., Hollywood's infamous "Rat Pack."

Perhaps the most dramatic result of Exner's Ghia concepts translated to Chrysler production models in 1957 with the totally redesigned 300C.

The entire Chrysler model line grew tailfins of monumental proportions that year, along with sleek, sporty bodylines that literally caught GM and Ford stylists with their collective pants down. Exner had swept away Chrysler's stodgy image in a single bold stroke but he had saved the very best for the 300C, distinguished from all other 1957 models by a massive grille that virtually consumed the front of the car. Based on an inverted rendition of the 1955 Ghia Falcon grille, the new edifice would become a Letter Car trademark through 1959, and influence Chrysler styling well into the 1960s.

The 1957 Chrysler 300C carried a 392-cubic-inch, 375-horsepower V-8 as standard equipment. Chrysler also offered an optional Speed Package that boosted output to a soul-stirring 390 horsepower. Production of the 300C coupe was limited to 1,918 cars. This was also the year Chrysler stylists took out the trimming shears and removed the top from the 300, releasing a mere 484 convertibles. This model is ranked today as one of the most desirable of all 1950s cars.

In 1958, Chrysler climbed the alphabet to D. The 300 was now equipped with a 392-cubic-inch engine rated at 380 horsepower in standard trim, and 390 with an optional Bendix electronic fuel-injection system. The injected 390 engine was exclusive to the Alphabet Cars and only offered in 1958. For the year, Chrysler produced a scant 191 300D convertibles, and of those, only 35 were equipped with the 390, making them a very rare find. The coupes were almost as rare, with orders for the 300D hardtops totaling only 618.

In 1959, only 140 Chrysler 300E convertibles and 550 hardtop coupes left the factory. This year the cars were equipped with a new 413-cubic-inch V-8 developing 380 horsepower. Chrysler closed the books on the 1950s with the introduction of the 1960 300F in the fall of 1959. An optional V-8 displacing 413 cubic inches and equipped with a Cross-ram induction manifold gave the car 400 horsepower and almost unchallenged domination of the American road.

Detroit closed out the first decade of the postwar era with an exceptional number of new and innovative designs. Not all were successful, but almost every one has become a reminder of a time when Detroit was the center of the world and the American automobile king of the road.

Although Chrysler had a powerful car in the 300B, many considered its styling too sedate. When the 1957 model year came around, Chrysler wrapped its improved 390-horsepower V-8 with a body that set Detroit and the rest of the automotive world on its ear. The all-new Chrysler 300C was not only the fastest stock sedan in the world, it was also the most modern looking as well.

THE BIG STEEL ERA BEGINS

CHAPTER 4

American Cars from 1950 to 1956

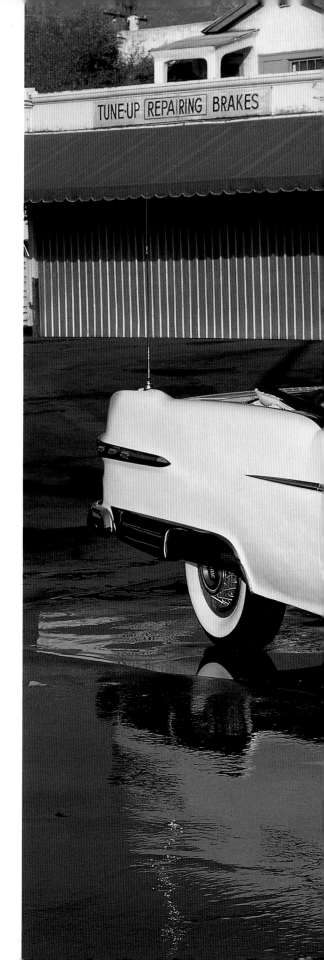

A s a nation of drivers we had been homebound since February 2, 1942, when civilian automobile production was halted and the last automobile, a Ford sedan, rolled off the River Rouge assembly line just ahead of the first B-24 bomber. After four long years of hardship, shortages of everything from tires to engine parts, gasoline rationing, and a 35-mile-per-hour national speed limit, it was no wonder Americans were making substantial deposits to get on waiting lists and paying under the table to purchase a new car in 1946, even if they were just restyled 1942 models.

In the few short years between 1946 and the first models of the new decade, the American automobile industry virtually reinvented itself. "It wasn't until about 1949 that really new cars started to appear," recalled retired GM design chief Chuck Jordan. "One of the first was the 1949 Ford and when I first saw that I said, 'Wow, look at that car. A Ford!'"

Jordan, who was only 22 when Harley Earl hired him at General Motors, said that there was a special passion for styling in the 1950s. "It had to do with the emotional quality that was in the design. The design of cars was very clear, it had character and personality, and we did this with passion, we felt very strongly about 'this is the way it ought to be,' and I think that is part of what came through. There was an excitement to the old cars, a certain elegance, a certain beauty."

If you ask Chuck Jordan, or just about any stylist who started with Detroit's Big Three during the postwar era, they'll all agree that it was much easier to design cars back in the 1950s. "And it was more fun," crows Jordan. "Harley Earl and Bill Mitchell were not only great designers, they were great leaders with an intuition, and when we designed a car it was whether *we* felt this was the right thing. We didn't take sketches out to product clinics and ask 150 people what they thought would be the best idea to use. Management relied on the talent of the designer."

Two-tone interiors to match the exterior color scheme were typical of Pontiac models produced in the early 1950s.

The 1955 Pontiacs were the division's first totally new postwar cars. Although all of the new GM models shared common styling cues, the Pontiac line was distinguished by its bumper and grille design, the use of distinctive fanjet-type crescents above the headlamps, and dual silver streaks, which started at the grille arch and ran to the cowl.

In 1955, the revolutionary new V-8-powered Chevrolet Bel Air challenged the industry-leading Ford V-8 for the first time ever. The new 90-degree Turbo-Fire V-8 delivered from 162 brake horsepower at 4,400 rpm up to 180 brake horsepower at 4,600 rpm when equipped with the "power-pack" option. As shown in these two photos, nothing remained of the 1954 Chevy model except the name and bow tie emblem. The 1955's wide grille opening, which observers were quick to note resembled the front of a Ferrari sports car, highlighted a list of styling cues that endowed every model from the sporty two-door hardtops and convertibles to the station wagons with a unique, aggressive appearance.

Pontiac's new two-barrel V-8 was originally offered with either standard or high-compression cylinder heads. The base engine had a compression ratio of 7.4:1 developing 173 horsepower at 4,400 rpm and 256 foot pounds of torque at 2,400 rpm. The high-compression (8.0:1) engine offered 180 horsepower at 4,600 revs and torque of 264 foot pounds at 2,400 rpm. This latter version was used in all cars equipped with HydraMatic transmissions. Later in the 1955 model year, Pontiac issued another, more powerful high-compression V-8 breathing through a four-barrel carb and delivering 200 horsepower.

One thing about the 1950s, it was a time when "brand new" actually implied something you had never seen before, like Cinemascope and stereophonic sound, introduced in 1953 with the film *From Here to Eternity.* "Limited production" had real meaning back then, too. Detroit automakers would actually tool up and produce a handful of special models. "We knew no boundaries, we had unlimited fuel, unlimited resources, the country was booming and industry was at an all-time high," remembered Jack Telnack, Ford Motor Company's vice president of corporate design. When Telnack joined Ford in 1958, he says styling was king. ". . . and I use the word *styling* not *design.* We had no government regulations back then. What we had was an incredible amount of energy and resources in this country, and the cars were an extension of that. We were redesigning cars every year and we didn't spend a lot of time on the understructure or running gear." Indeed, it seemed as if annual sheet metal changes and increasing horsepower were the only changes that mattered.

The American motorist was truly the greatest benefactor of World War II. Readily available domestic oil, processed by great refineries and transported through mammoth pipelines that had been built during the war, resulted in a glut of inexpensive gasoline and a proliferation of company-owned filling stations, one on almost every corner. The automobile had become

king of the road and by the early 1950s General Motors had secured its place in the American automotive industry as the maker of kings.

With five divisions, GM produced as many as or more cars than all of its competitors combined. The corporate architect of General Motors, Alfred P. Sloan,

who took the helm from founder William C. Durant in the 1920s, had foreseen a day when automobile ownership would be defined by age, income, and class. By the 1950s, General Motors had established its own caste system, a product for every income and every rung of the social ladder.

At the entry level there was Chevrolet, priced low enough for the average worker to afford. It was, as GM viewed it, the first step in a long relationship that would see owners trade up as they grew in age and financial stature.

For those who had ascended to middle management and were confident about their financial future, the Pontiac Division offered a sportier, more prestigious line of cars and by the mid-1950s, Pontiac would share with Chevrolet, GM's strongest front to attract youthful buyers.

GM had purposefully created its own brand of one-upmanship, so that no matter what model you were driving there was always another to seed greater aspirations until you reached the top. Oldsmobile was the third rung in GM's socioeconomic ladder. The standard

The fourth of GM's 1953 Motorama Dream Cars, the Corvette was so well received that dealers demanded a 1953 model. Chevrolet complied by producing 300 Polo White roadsters with red interiors. The car pictured is the prototype shown at the 1953 New York Motorama. Author collection

barer of the executive set, it was closely followed by Buick, the car for bankers, lawyers, doctors and corporate executives. Finally, there was Cadillac, America's most prestigious automotive name. In the GM hierarchy, Cadillac was for captains of industry, stars of stage and screen, top corporate executives and the president of the United States. By the end of the 1950s, the goals envisioned by Alfred P. Sloan some 25 years earlier had been realized. Ford, Chrysler and the lot of American automakers could only stand back and watch with admiration GM's overwhelming command of the industry. Harley Earl and the Detroit establishment were essentially dictating what Americans wanted in a new car.

In 1953, General Motors introduced four distinctive, very limited production convertibles, the Cadillac Eldorado, Buick Skylark, Oldsmobile Fiesta and Chevrolet Corvette, all of which were produced in the hundreds rather than in the thousands and tens of thousands.

Nineteen-fifty three was also a benchmark year for the Oldsmobile division as the four-millionth Oldsmobile rolled off the Lansing assembly line on May 12. The general styling of the 1953 models was carried over from the previous year with the Olds' design staff focusing its efforts on a new instrument panel, new bumpers and new exterior trim. Overall, exterior styling hadn't changed dramatically since the first Futuramic Rocket V-8s introduced in 1949. Most of the emphasis between 1949 and 1953 was on the rear fender design. The most striking change of all was

the demise of the sporty fastback sedans after 1950.

Oldsmobile's overall look was bolder, featuring a new front bumper integrated with the grille. The bumper guards were bent inward to follow the contour of the grille frame, and they carried pods resembling turbojet engine cowlings on top, linked together by a horizontal bar. A similar appearance graced the front view of nearly all GM models in 1953, as Harley Earl and the GM design studio enhanced their aircraft-inspired "power styling" cues.

A few minor changes in body trim, rear fender sculpturing and a new contour for the rear decklid gave the 1953 models a fresh silhouette and the illusion of additional length. As Earl was to confess a year later, "My primary purpose for twenty-eight years has been to lengthen and lower the American automobile, at times in reality, and always at least in appearance."

While the exterior looked very much the same, from behind the wheel, the 1953 Olds models were completely different with a new instrument panel design that reprised the full-circle speedometer, positioned directly in front of the driver. To compliment it, the passenger side duplicated the speedometer design with a circle of equal size, filled by a grooved dish containing the radio speaker and a small clock. The glove box was positioned in the center of the dashboard, with a radio tucked neatly into the trim above it.

The model lineup for 1953, the Deluxe 88, Super 88 and top-of-the-line Ninety-Eight, offered a full range of body styles from sedate four-door sedans

The most common Fiesta color combination was Surf Blue and Teal Blue. Noel and Nile green were also offered, as were solid white and black. Interiors were finished in green, blue, or black hand-buffed leather trimmed with ivory. Although some Fiestas have been found with continental kits, they were a dealer-installed option.

The Fiesta shared its rakishly low beltline and wraparound windshield with the Buick Skylark and Cadillac Eldorado in 1953. The spinner wheel covers soon became an Olds tradition.

to sporty two-door hardtops and convertibles, the soft tops carrying a hefty price of $2,615 for the Super 88 and $2,963 for the Ninety-Eight.

Keeping pace with Cadillac, which offered the exclusive Eldorado as a limited production model in 1953, Oldsmobile introduced its own special limited-edition luxury convertible—the Fiesta. Originally, it had been a 1952 Auto Show "idea car" showcasing such innovations as the "panoramic" windshield first used on the Eldorado. The Fiesta received so much attention that Olds management decided to put it into limited production during the 1953 model year, although it was never pictured in any Oldsmobile sales literature, except for an oversized green-tone postcard devoted exclusively to the car. Only 458 Olds Fiestas were produced, making it one of the rarest postwar American cars.

Loaded with just about every option in the book, the Fiesta came with a slightly souped-up 170-horse-power version of the Quadri-Jet Rocket V-8, Hydra-Matic transmission and a whopping $5,715 price tag, almost twice as much as the base price for an Olds Ninety-Eight convertible!

For the money, the Fiesta came with a custom leather-upholstered interior, Hydra-Matic, power steering, power brakes, electric windows, power seats, Autronic-eye automatic headlamp dimming, whitewalls, radio/heater and more.

At a glance, the Fiesta appeared to be a dressed up Ninety-Eight convertible with a wraparound wind-shield but the car was actually some three inches lower

Loaded with just about every option in the book, the Fiesta's slightly souped-up version of the Quadri-Jet Rocket V-8 turned out 170 horsepower.

than the standard model.

The Fiesta was offered in a choice of four colors. Solids were black and white, with two-tone options in Noel and Nile Green, and surf and teal blue. Other combinations were added later in the model year. Although a continental-style spare was not a factory option, a few of the cars were equipped with the rear-mounted tires by Oldsmobile dealers. It was a cumbersome affair that made access to the trunk awkward at best. Still, the look was in vogue and convenience often took a back seat to style.

Banner years are few and far between in the auto industry, especially for General Motors divisions which compete against each other for market share. In 1955, however, it was great to be Olds, as GM's near luxury marque posted its best year in nearly 60 years of operation, establishing a sales record that would stand for a decade. For the model year a whopping 583,179 cars found their way into American garages making Oldsmobile the number four automaker in the country.

Oldsmobile's record-breaking year came on the heels of a model line that had been restyled in 1954 and only slightly updated for 1955. The most obvious and attractive change was the deep set and chrome trimmed headlights. Other styling changes included new side moldings, new front and rear emblems—a revised Ringed-World design that was only used on 1955 models—and the extension of the sweep cut front fenders to the 88 and Super 88 Series, matching 1954 Ninety-Eight Series styling.

Harley Earl's 1955 Oldsmobile models featured a full-oval grille inspired by jet aircraft used in Korea, such as North American's F-86 Sabre. The menacing Oldsmobile grille was the car's most distinguishing feature.

Although Oldsmobile still designed its own frames, suspensions, steering systems, engines and drivetrains, the total concept was dictated by GM Corporate, with divisions sharing common body designs which were distinguished by grilles, lights and trim. The Olds' model line was built on the GM "B" body also shared with the Buick division.

The lower, longer-looking designs of the 1954 and 1955 model years were made possible in part by the use of a new V-8 engine being introduced throughout GM, which had a lower profile than its inline, vertical predecessor. The new V-8 allowed

Behind the wheel in a Fiesta, it was easy to find the speedometer. The dashboard featured a padded protective cover. The cars had special leather upholstery and color-keyed, checked carpeting. Standard features included power steering and brakes, super deluxe radio, Autronic Eye, and a heater/defroster. Pleated two-tone leather interior was typical of 1955 Oldsmobiles. Leather was standard on the Super 88 convertible, and two-toning to match the exterior paint was not uncommon.

Packing 202 horsepower, the 1955 Rocket
V-8 featured a new camshaft with higher-
lift cam lobes and a revised combustion
chamber design increasing compression
ratio to 8.5:1. With 202 horses under the
hood, the Super 88 was clocked by
Motor Trend at a top speed of 106 miles
per hour and covered the standing start
quarter mile in 18.1 seconds.

The Olds Super 88 instrument panel was
a visual knockout with big instruments
and chrome, chrome, chrome!

Harley Earl's 1955 Oldsmobile models
featured a full-oval grille inspired by jet
aircraft used in Korea, such as North
American's F-86 Sabre. The menacing
Oldsmobile grille was the car's most
distinguishing feature. The shorter
wheelbase of the Super 88 wasn't
apparent in the convertible model thanks
to the Olds' lower, longer bodylines.

Earl's stylists to pen body designs which would bring
hoodlines down, while at the same time enabling GM
engineers to bring horsepower ratings up. The Rocket
V-8 for 1955 featured a new camshaft with higher-lift
cam lobes and a revised combustion chamber design
contributing to an increased compression ratio of
8.5:1. Output for the top-of-the-line Rocket V-8s
would jump to 202 horsepower. And for the first
time, the higher-rated engine could also be ordered as
a $35 option on any Olds 88 model.

As tested by *Motor Trend* in April 1955, the Super
88 clocked 0 to 60 in 11.8 seconds, recorded a top speed
of 106 miles per hour, and covered the standing start
quarter mile in 18.1 seconds.

The 1955 Oldsmobiles were not only faster but
better handling as well, with a completely redesigned

Interior of the Buick Skylark was luxuriously appointed. Note the Skylark name on the door sill.

The Buick Skylark was number three in GM's Triple Crown—Cadillac Eldorado, and Oldsmobile Fiesta being one and two. The flighty name for Buick's dream car came from a song of the same name recorded in 1942 by Johnny Mercer, then again by Dick Haymes, Woody Herman, Gene Krupa, and Billy Eckstein. No wonder GM chose the name, everyone had already heard it! Production in 1953 and again in 1954 was limited, but the image Buick portrayed with the Skylark carried through to the entire product line.

independent-type front suspension system called "Power Ride." The new independent front suspension (IFS) design utilized telescopic shock absorbers mounted for the first time *inside* the coil springs. The rear suspension on all 1955 Oldsmobiles consisted of two 2x58-inch leaf springs and angle-mounted, direct-acting shock absorbers. Front and rear stabilizer bars were used to improve handling, as was an improved manual steering gear, and the adoption of 15-inch tubeless tires for all series. Supplied by Firestone, U.S. Royal, and B.F. Goodrich, the standard Super 88 tire size was 7.60x15 inches with an oversize tire measuring 8.00x15 inches available as an option.

Oldsmobile's "Go Ahead" look for 1955 was highlighted by the sporty top-of-the-line Series 88 convertible. Available only as a Super 88 model, prices for the luxuriously equipped convertibles started at $2,894 but few left the showrooms for under $3,000, making this the most expensive car in the 88 series. Rarest among all

1955 Oldsmobiles, it was designated model number 553667DTX, and production totaled only 9,007.

The Super 88 was one of only two open cars available in the 1955 Olds lineup. The other was the Ninety-Eight Starfire Convertible. This graceful model was designated 553067 DX and was Oldsmobile's most expensive offering, with a hefty $3,276 window sticker.

A total of 10 solid colors were available for the Super 88 convertible including Glen Green, Juneau Gray, Coral, Bronze Metallic, and Burlingame Red, along with 10 special two-tone combinations. All convertibles featured leather interiors in either solids or two-tone combinations and top colors of the recommended black, tan, green, blue, white Toptex and white orlon—a $50 extra. The cars could also be special ordered with a rigid fiberglass top boot—a la Cadillac Eldorado—a $95 option; another $50 added deluxe hubcaps on 88 and Super 88 models.

Inside the new Oldsmobiles, both the standard and deluxe steering wheels were redone. Each had a new recessed hub design with the world emblem in the center. The 1955 dash had new, clean, smooth surfaces with chrome control knobs. The instrument cluster, radio dial, speaker grille and panel molding on the 88 Series were now chrome, the same as all other series in 1954. Carpeting was made standard on Super 88s and optional on all 88 models.

The newest power accessory added to the 1955 option list was a power-operated radio antenna listing for $20. Two radio options were available, the deluxe radio—six tubes, push button tuning—could be installed for $94.50. The super deluxe radio—8 tubes, signal seeking and favorite station tuning—was $121 installed. Other factory options included an electric clock, rear radio speaker, electric windows and tinted glass.

Compared to the big Ninety-Eight, the Super 88 rode a four-inch shorter wheelbase and weighed about 150-200 pounds less. Since it had the same engine, with 17-horsepower more than the base 88, it was the quickest and nimblest Oldsmobile model for 1955. It was also the most popular, available in five different models—convertible, two-door sedan, Holiday coupe, four-door sedan and Holiday sedan—accounting for well over 200,000 sales in the 1955 model year and over 150,000 in 1956.

Sales were so good in 1955 that a multi-million dollar expansion effort was begun in June to double the Lansing operation's production capacity. The 1955 model year also marked another Olds milestone: production of the division's five-millionth car, which rolled off the Lansing assembly line in July.

Some automobiles were naturals. They were a hit before the model ever reached the showroom floor. The 1955 Pontiac Star Chief convertible was one of those cars.

The 1955 Pontiacs were the division's first totally new postwar model. Although all of the new GM lines shared common styling cues, Pontiacs were distinguished by their bumper and grille designs and the use of distinctive fanjet-type crescents above the headlamps (a design derived from the Pontiac Strato Streak and Strato show cars) and dual silver streaks, (adopted from the Bonneville Special show car) which started at the grille arch and ran over the hood to the windshield. Chrome trim was used along the bottom of the rear fenders, and optional chromed skirts added a stylish accent to the rear wheel wells.

The horizontal impact bars used on 1955 models were replaced with round bumper guards in 1956, and the rectangular parking lights changed to round lamps built right into the lower bumper. At the other end, the 1956 models had longer rear fenders than the 1955's, adding an extra 2.4 inches to overall length. Both model years featured distinctive two-tone paint schemes.

Overall, the new Pontiac line, and the Star Chief convertible in particular, had shed the bulky look of the 1940s. With a hoodline lowered by 3.75 inches, bringing the fenders right up to the level of the hood, and a reduction in overall vehicle height of 2.75 inches, compared to 1954 models, the new cars appeared crisp, clean, and strikingly modern. The most significant change in 1955, however, was what Pontiac had packed beneath that new, lower hood!

By 1955 General Motors had summed up its corporate philosophy on performance with one symbol: V-8. Be it an affordable Chevrolet Bel Air, a top-of-the-line Cadillac Eldorado, Oldsmobile Super 88, Buick Roadmaster, or Pontiac Star Chief, GM had a V-8 engine available behind every grille.

Positioned at the lower end of the price scale, Chevrolet and Pontiac were the last GM divisions to introduce V-8s. At Pontiac, the new 287-cubic-inch, overhead-valve V-8 engine replaced both the sixes and old 268-cubic-inch in-line eights. (Chevy kept its six-cylinder engines for base models.)

Pontiac's new two-barrel V-8 was originally offered with either standard or high-compression cylinder heads. The base engine had a compression ratio of 7.4:1 developing 173 horsepower at 4,400 rpm and 256 foot pounds of torque at 2,400. The high-compression engine, with an 8.0:1 ratio, bumped output to 180 horsepower at 4,600 revs and torque to 264 foot pounds at 2,400 rpm. This version was used in all cars equipped with HydraMatic transmissions. Later in the 1955 model year, Pontiac issued another, more powerful high-compression V-8 breathing through a four-barrel carb and delivering 200 horsepower. This engine also came outfitted with a heavy-duty air cleaner and a low-restriction intake manifold. The bump in price for the

optional four barrel was $30. For the money, you got a throatier exhaust note, and a full second off the 0 to 60 time. (The 180-horsepower engines averaged 13.8 seconds, the 200 horsepower 12.7, according to a 1955 *Motor Trend* comparison test.)

On the engineering side, the 1955 Pontiacs were built atop a modified frame with straight side members and new cross bracing adapted to carry the V-8 and match up with new front and rear suspension systems. On the steering end, Pontiac employed a new independent design with vertical kingpins, coil springs and A-arms, combined with a new recirculating-ball steering gear and parallelogram linkage. The solid axle rear used fewer, but longer, leaf springs mounted 3.25 inches further apart than on 1954 models, thus forming a wider, more stable base. Pontiac's new underpinnings also included larger front brakes, increased to a 12-inch diameter, with the rears remaining at 11 inches. Tubeless tires were made standard on all models, as was a 12-volt electrical system.

Pontiac had designed its "Strato Streak" V-8 so that increases in displacement could be made without extensive retooling. What was already good in 1955 got better in 1956. The engines were enlarged to 317 cubic inches, with outputs raised to 205 horsepower and 227 horsepower, respectively. The 1956 models were also equipped with a new "Strato-Flight" HydraMatic, designed to han-

The "new" Eldorado became a luxury version of the Series 62 convertible. Of the standard convertible coupes, priced at $4,404, Cadillac sold a total of 6,310. The premium Eldorado, at $1,300 more, gave owners the distinctive name and gold emblems, broad ribbed chrome panels on the lower rear fenders, a luxuriously appointed leather interior, and chromed wire wheels.

In 1954, the Eldorado became a brand-new model in the Cadillac lineup. Although it had been introduced in 1953 as a special, limited, almost custom-built edition, as a production model in 1954, the stylish convertible was changed considerably from the Motorama version sold in 1953.

After the 1954 Eldorado, Cadillac needed to do something even more spectacular, and the 1955 version was Bill Mitchell's first monument to the Harley Earl-inspired tailfin. The only 1955 model to be restyled, the Eldorado got boldly styled "rocketship" tailfins three years before the rest of the Cadillac model line. The new fins featured dual taillights (one taillight and backup light per side). In 1955, Eldos had their own exclusive engine, a 270-horsepower version of the 331-cubic-inch V-8 with dual four-barrel carburetion. A record 3,950 Eldorados were sold in 1955.

dle the increased torque and shift smoother.

The 1955 and 1956 Pontiacs were, in their own right, significant new models, bringing the division out of the 1940s and well on the road to breaking from its long established image as a conservative-looking car. A boom in 1955 model sales put 530,007 Pontiacs in American garages. While much of their new-found popularity could be attributed to modern body styling and V-8 performance, Pontiac's affordable pricing, starting at $1,917.45 for the Chieftain two-door sedan and running up to $2,462 for the Star Chief convertible, certainly didn't hurt.

Much to Pontiac's surprise and total dismay, sales in 1957 tumbled to 358,668 cars, dropping Pontiac's share of the new car market to only 6.02 percent, and a solid fourth place behind Chevrolet, Buick and Oldsmobile. That, however, was nothing to be ashamed of. Pontiac's contribution helped put GM over the top, with total divisional sales accounting for 50.7 percent of every new American car sold in the United States!

As for Pontiac itself, image remained a problem through the late 1950s. With only the Star Chief as a styling leader, the rest of the model line failed to attract younger, more affluent buyers. Pontiacs were still perceived as the car your dad drove, despite the styling changes and performance gains. However, all that was about to change under the leadership of Pontiac's new General Manager, Semon "Bunkie" Knudsen. His influence on Pontiac, from 1956 to 1961, would take the division to the number three spot in the industry.

For Buick, times had been favorable since the late 1940s. The division had found itself in the enviable position, come 1945, of having cars that were not dated in appearance. America's involvement in the war had come just as Buick introduced an entirely new model line, so warmed-over 1942s really weren't *that* warmed-over. Buick's new chief of design, Ned Nickels, had done a standout job of facelifting the 1942 sheet metal and adding just enough pizazz to the early postwar models to move Buick into the number five spot in total new car sales.

Between 1945 and 1953, when the Buick Skylark was introduced, a styling revolution had taken place in America. The age of chrome and fins had arrived. Though Cadillac was to take that theme to the height of absurdity, Buick's approach was more restrained.

Throughout the early 1950s the basic lines of the postwar Buicks had gently matured under the guiding eye of Ned Nickels. The 1953 and 1954 Skylarks were transitory, carrying the last quantifiable traits of the 1940s—the sweeping "Airfoil" fenderline, rear kickup, the prominent hood height and bold grille, giving way to the smooth integrated bodylines of the 1950s. Yet, there were some styling traits which translated well into the new look, carrying forth recognizable and well-established postwar Buick character lines. The most notable were seen in the grille and headlights. The headlights went virtually unchanged, and the grille, though narrower, contained more bars. While the 1954 models at once rendered the 1953s and all earlier Buicks old-fashioned, the 1954s clearly showed the road from whence they had come.

The 1953 Skylark, priced at $4,595 was the most lavishly optioned Buick produced to that time. It offered power brakes, power steering, power windows, power seats, and a power antenna for the foot-controlled Selectronic radio. Built on the Roadmaster chassis, the Skylark was planned for only a single year's production. Like the 1953 Eldorado, the Skylark was a specially produced model with a body designed to offer lower, sportier lines than the rest of each division's respective offerings. With its top raised, the Skylark stood less than five feet tall—low for 1953.

Styling for the 1953 Skylark centered around the cut-down doorline, notched beltline, and the sweeps-pear chrome trim following the shape of the fenders and rising upward to accent the bold, cutout rear wheel openings. It was, by all comparison, a successful model, a fanciful, sporty two-door that not only accomplished its primary task—to attract customers into the show-room—but also sold surprisingly well, recording 1,690 sales. While some authorities say that the 1953 Skylark is more desirable than the 1954, it's all a matter of opinion. First of all, the 1954 was never planned. It was an encore at the behest of Harley Earl. Since the entire 1954 Buick model line was new, the Skylark had to be completely redesigned for a single model year run!

The 1954 Skylark was built on the Century convertible chassis (not nearly as exclusive a platform as the 1953 had), with a wheelbase some 3.5 inches shorter. And for the most part, a great deal of the Skylark's distinctive styling surfaced throughout the entire Buick line, including the new Panoramic windshield (introduced in 1953 on the Cadillac Eldorado), unskirted rear wheels, pseudo cut down doors, and the bold chromed sweeps-pear trim running the length of the body.

What distinguished the Skylark from the Century was Nickles' ability to create different looks with minimal changes. The front and rear wheel cutouts were drawn back, exposing the inner panels, a design inspired by the 1953 Buick Wildcat and 1954 Buick Wildcat II Motorama show cars. The panels were painted red on white cars and white on darker hued Skylarks, to contrast the body color. The overall effect was very dramatic no matter what color combination buyers selected. At the rear, the fenderline had a stylish downward curve matching the shape of the wheel openings, and well-defined chromed tailfins completed the Skylark's distinctive profile. The trunk lid was the final styling element, featuring what Buick described as a "corsair-sweep," a somewhat unusual design which extended the shape of the rear bumper guards upward into the body. Last, Buick badged the Skylarks with a bold bird-in-flight emblem and replaced the popular gun sight hood ornament with a specially designed version featuring a series of circles and a large "V" at the center. As a final departure from the rest of the Buick line, the traditional front fender portholes were eliminated.

Under the long stretch of hood, Buick loaded the Skylark with the Roadmaster's 200-horsepower Fire-ball V-8, coupled to a Twin-Turbine Dynaflow automatic transmission. The 1954 models again offered the full complement of power features as standard equipment and wide whitewall tires mounted on special 15x6-inch Kelsey-Hayes chrome-plated wire wheels.

Chrome embellishments were the defining characteristic of the Crown Victoria which had a wide chrome bar extending over the roof, the "crown" if you will, which was also repeated on the inside headliner.

The Ford Crown Victoria was a two-year model run, discontinued in 1957, but for two years it reigned as the flashiest version of the commonest car, a special version of the everyman's Fairlane coupe.

By 1953, Lincoln was building a new image as a manufacturer of high-performance luxury cars, cars that could win races. In 1953, a new Lincoln won the stock car class in the grueling Carrera Panamericana road race for the second year in a row. In addition, Cosmopolitan Custom Sport Coupes captured second, third, and fourth positions. In 1954 and again in 1955, Lincoln repeated its class win in Mexico. Pictured is one of the Lincolns that ran in the fifth Carrera Panamericana.

While Buick referred to the Skylark in its 1954 sales brochure as a "sports car," that was stretching things a bit. Built on a double-drop X-braced frame, the Skylark had an independent coil spring front suspension and a semi-floating rear axle. The car had great styling, quick acceleration, but a soft, floating ride and the cornering ability of a Chris Craft. The Skylark was anything but a sports car.

Only 798 Skylarks were built in 1954, enough to again draw people into Buick showrooms, many of whom drove out in a more affordable Century convertible, Buick Super, Buick Special or Roadmaster, putting GM's near luxury badge in the number three spot for total new car sales in 1954.

Even before the war, Cadillac had firmly established itself as America's luxury leader. Crosstown rivals Lincoln and Packard were both struggling with their postwar images having failed to regain the sales momentum they had before the war.

In 1954, the Eldorado became a brand-new model. Although it had been introduced in 1953 as a special, limited, almost custom-built edition, when it became a production model, the stylish convertible was changed considerably from the Motorama version sold the previous year. Cadillac restyled the entire lineup for 1954 and the Eldorado became a luxury version of the Series 62 convertible.

For the first time in four years, Cadillac had made a major styling change, and all of the 1954s more or less echoed the look of the 1953 Eldorado, with its wraparound Panoramic windshield, higher, more fully integrated fenders, lower hoodline, and longer, wider rear deck. The 1954 coupes and sedans also introduced a wide wraparound rear window to complement the windshield and all three model lines, Series Sixty-Two, Fleetwood Sixty Special, and Fleetwood Seventy-Five, rode on longer wheelbases, each increased by three inches from the previous year.

In redesigning the Cadillac, Harley Earl, Bill Mitchell, and the styling department had come up with a few new and very interesting twists to the Caddy's famous grillework. The new grille had a distinctive upper and lower section and integrated bumpers and chromed bumper guards, the latter design earning the rather descriptive nickname "Dagmars" in honor of a similarly endowed actress of the era.

When they first came out in 1950, Cadillac's combined ornament and bumper guards had been dubbed "bullets" and in 1953, when they became even larger, they were elevated in stature to "grille bombs." Never had so much attention been paid to naming a single automotive attribute.

Behind all the brightwork, Cadillac underscored its new front end with a distinctive horizontal "eggcrate" grille that would become de rigueur in one form or another well into the late 1950s.

Perhaps one of the reasons Cadillacs were so popular back in the early postwar years, was that few automakers offered as many variations on the luxury car theme; there were a total of eight body styles from which to choose. Of the standard convertible coupes, priced at $4,404, Cadillac sold a total of 6,310. The premium Eldorado at $1,300 more gave owners the distinctive name and gold emblems, broad ribbed chrome panels on the lower rear fenders, a luxuriously appointed leather interior and chromed wire wheels.

Cadillac offered the Eldorado in four special colors, Aztec Red, Azure Blue, Apollo Gold, and Alpine White. A total of 2,150 were built. Not as rare as the 1953 models, but hardly mass production, either.

Across town in Dearborn, Ford Motor Company was doing its best to counter the highly successful Chevrolet Bel Air. In 1955 Ford sold more than 1.5 million cars. Of that number 33,164 were Crown Victorias, the new Ford flagship.

The Crown Victoria was a two-year model run, discontinued in 1957, but for two years it reigned as the flashiest version of a most common car, a special rendering of the everyman's Fairlane coupe.

Chrome embellishments were the defining characteristic of both the Fairlane and the Crown Victoria which added a wide chrome bar extending over the roof, the "crown" if you will, which was also repeated on the inside headliner. The Crown Victoria was offered either in standard trim or with the optional Skyliner tinted plexiglass roof section up front. Base price for the Crown Victoria was $2,302 f.o.b. Detroit.

Thanks to the sweeping Fairlane trim—an elongated "Vee form" speedline which began as a solid chrome strip at the back of the headlights, followed along the fenders, dropped down into a deep V through the doors, and then divided into four separate lines dashing straight back along the fenders to the taillights—Ford found it easy to offer the cars with two-tone paint schemes.

Ford had achieved something of a milestone in 1955 with the introduction of the Thunderbird. The two-seater's first year success had turned the automotive spotlight in Ford's direction, at least long enough to steal some of the thunder from Chevrolet's all-new and beautifully styled V-8-powered Bel Air. Quick to capitalize on the Thunderbird's notoriety, Ford placed a stylized Thunderbird insignia on the front fenders of the Fairlane and Crown Victoria models and equipped them with a 292-cubic-inch, 202-horsepower, "Y-Block" Thunderbird Special V-8.

The Lincoln division was doing well with the luxurious Cosmopolitan, which had become the marque's flagship after the Continental's demise in 1948. By 1956, Lincoln was on its way to challenging Cadillac once again. The completely redesigned Premiere, available in two- and four-door models and a convertible, was a handsome car by anyone's standards. The stylish

Lincoln Premiere coupe attracted 19,619 buyers, the sedan another 19,465 sales and the convertible an additional 2,447 new Lincoln owners.

Ironically, it wasn't Cadillac that upstaged Lincoln's 1956 model year, it was Lincoln itself with the introduction of a car intended to not only rival GM's luxury marque but surpass it. It was the Continental Mark II, an automobile so distinctive that it totally redefined the image of American luxury cars. More than 30 years later it is still regarded as one of the most significant designs of the 1950s.

Lincoln heralded the Continental Mk II's arrival as the "Rebirth of a Proud Tradition." It was, in fact, much more, at least from a historical perspective.

The prestigious Continental name had been absent from the Lincoln line for eight years, but moreover, so too had the handcrafted workmanship that made the original 1940 Continental an almost custom-built car. Mass production had become the order of business by

1956. Detroit assembly lines were turning out automobiles in record numbers; but to manufacture the Continental Mk II, Ford returned to the old handcrafted ways.

The cars were almost entirely custom-built according to exacting standards and material specifications, making the Continental Mk II the most expensive mass-produced car ever offered for sale up to that time. Priced at $9,695, it was as close as any American automaker in the 1950s would ever come to building a car in the classic 1930s tradition.

The sleek four-passenger coupe had an overall height of just 56 inches, a length of 218.5 inches on a 126-inch wheelbase, and a width of 77.5 inches. The classic proportions of a long hood, short mid-section, and rear deck—incorporating a modern interpretation of the original Continental spare—were penned by the team of John Reinhart and legendary Auburn, Cord, Duesenberg designer Gordon Buehrig. The distinctive styling of the Continental is considered by many to be

By 1956, Lincoln was on the way to challenging Cadillac once again. The completely redesigned Premiere, available in two- and four-door models and a convertible, was a handsome car by anyone's standards. The stylish Lincoln Premiere coupe attracted 19,619 buyers, the sedan another 19,465 customers, and the convertible an additional 2,447 new Lincoln owners.

59

As the land yacht of the 1940s headed for dry dock, wood became a less common feature. This 1950 Chrysler Town & Country Newport shows how little of the original concept remained. Only the white ash outer framework is still used and rather than having the bodies coachbuilt, the wood is merely bolted onto the steel body panels.

the 1950s equivalent of Buehrig's hallmark 1936 Cord 810, another design that clearly stood head-and-shoulders above the competition.

Lincoln had at last outdone Cadillac by creating a car so stunning in its appearances, so luxuriously appointed and calculatedly limited in production, as to be without equal.

At the outset, Continental was organized as a new division of Ford Motor Company with its own operations and an exclusive assembly plant in Ecorse Township, Michigan. The Mk II was built on a special chassis frame unlike any being used on production Lincolns. The powertrain, aside from a unique drive-shaft arrangement, was comprised of Lincoln components that were hand picked. The engine was a 368-cubic-inch ohv V-8 specially tuned to deliver an estimated 285 horsepower, although the Continental Division never officially disclosed the Mk II's horsepower—a Rolls-Royce marketing trait that Lincoln smartly appropriated.

Ford Motor Company had estimated that a break even point of 2,500 units per year was necessary to make the Continental profitable, but given the complexity of manufacturing the car that number soon became unrealistic. As a cost-saving measure instituted in July 1956, the Continental Division was incorporated into the Lincoln Division.

The Mk II was only produced for two years; however, there is no actual 1956 or 1957 model year designation. The Continental was considered a model series, although cars built between June 1955 and September 1956 were registered as 1956 models and those built thereafter were technically considered 1957s. Total production is estimated to be 2,989 units, and with 23 prototypes added, including one convertible built for William Clay Ford, a grand total of 3,012 Continentals were built.

Like the rest of Detroit's automakers, Chrysler had emerged from the war in good financial shape. For 1950, production moved up to 167,316 for the calendar year, the best sales record since 1928. Chrysler moved ahead of Hudson, Kaiser-Frazer, Cadillac, Packard, Lincoln and Willys.

Chrysler had overhauled its product lines in 1949 and there were few changes in 1950 except for a new hardtop model called the Newport and the addition of power windows as an option on all eight-cylinder models. Nineteen-fifty marked the end of the Town & Country model line, which was now limited to a two-door hardtop. A run of only 698 woodies brought down the curtain on one of the postwar era's most interesting automotive styles, and Chrysler, like every other automaker in the country, was hard at work designing and engineering a new generation of automobiles that would appear in the mid-1950s.

CHROME, GLORIOUS CHROME

CHAPTER 5

Detroit Weighs in with Tonnage: 1957 to 1959

It's funny how time alters our perception of the past. Take American cars of the 1950s for example. People look at them today and say, "Wow! What magnificent automobiles." They get excited over every compound curve of the fenders, rave over the massive grillework, outsize bumpers, and all that wonderful chrome trim. They reminisce about the good old days when cars had character and didn't all look alike. You can't argue there, but we forget how poorly they handled, how much gas they consumed, and how we discarded them as old junkers when the next new thing came along. That's the beauty of looking back, we only remember the good parts.

American cars produced in the late 1950s were the most ostentatious to ever come from Detroit's styling studios. The big chrome look which had started tastefully in 1954 had reached almost absurd proportions by 1958, and GM models were bearers of the most glitz.

That people stayed away from GM showrooms in droves wasn't particularly the fault of General Motors' obsession with chrome and trim, but more the economy which had reached a dismal low by 1958, plunging the nation into the worst recession in years. Every American automaker was suffering, but General Motors, being the largest, seemed to be bearing the brunt of it. GM had lost better than 5 percent of its market share, falling from a dominating 50.7 percent. Although GM still accounted for nearly half the new cars sold in America, "nearly" was not good enough, particularly in 1958. It was General Motors' 50th anniversary, and nobody wanted to celebrate.

The demand for newer, more dramatic designs each year and the keen competition that had developed between American automakers was putting an incredible strain on stylists. By 1958 it had reached a point where styling was almost irrelevant to function. The wilder a design was,

So much of what Detroit created in the 1950s seems larger than life today—although at 40 inches above the road, maybe the 1959 Cadillac's tailfin was already larger than life! The creation of GM stylist Dave Holls, this visage of the Eldorado has become the icon of an American era.

The 1959 Eldorado was the most opulent overstatement in chrome and fins ever. Regardless of the model, every Cadillac had massive chrome-edged fins rearing up from just behind the doors, and sweeping skyward. The 1959 Eldorado Biarritz has become the quintessential motoring icon of the 1950s.

Pontiac's new flagship model, the Bonneville convertible, was chosen as the Official Pace Car of the 1958 Indianapolis 500 Mile Race. The Pontiac Pacesetter was driven by 1957's 500 Mile winner Sam Hanks.

It may well have been the need to attract buyers back into the showroom in 1958 that compelled corporate stylists to breech the boundaries of sensible proportions and create designs which almost mocked the outrageousness of their Motorama Dream Cars. Nevertheless, cars like the 1958 Bonneville Sport Coupe were attractive, if not overwhelming automobiles.

Inside, the 1958 Bonneville had a stylish new instrument panel featuring a "deep-cove" design with a textured aluminum fascia and chromed "stand-out" instruments. The upholstery was Patrician-patterned, nylon-faced Lustrex tapestry, combined with jewel-tone Morrokide trim. The example pictured is Burma Green with Calypso Green roof and side panel accents. The interior is the optional jewel-tone Morrokide and leather with Patrician tapestry weave Lustrex, all in a matching combination of two-tone green.

the bigger the car, the brighter the chrome, the better it appeared. The late Eugene Bordinat, who was responsible for some of Ford's most stunning designs in the 1950s, once remarked that people wanted chrome, "and we slathered them with it. Good taste had nothing to do with it whatsoever." It was an era best described as the triumph of style over substance.

By the late 1950s, Detroit was on a mission, a mission to reinvent the automobile every year, to make the 1957 models which had been trendsetters compared to the 1956 line, seem outdated by 1958. This had been the goal of General Motors design chief Harley Earl, to get Americans out of perfectly good cars and into brand-new ones by continually improving the design and making the car in our driveway seem hopelessly out of date. As Halberstam aptly noted, "Harley Earl was the standard bearer of the new age of affluence and abundance. It is possible that no one exerted as much influence on American style and taste in the fifties as he, and no one reflected more accurately what the country had become."

Tearing a page from his own past, Earl, who had designed custom coachwork for the Don Lee studio in Los Angeles before being recruited by Sloan and

Cadillac President Lawrence Fisher in 1926, recognized the automobile as more than a means of transportation. To Earl it was a fashion statement. "To change the car every year was our goal," recalled Chuck Jordan. "It was change for the sake of change, but we loved it and so did America." People lined up to get their first look at the new models each year. Dealers papered over their showroom windows to pique curiosity and the GM Motorama was a family event as eagerly awaited each year as the Ice Capades or the Ringling Bros., Barnum and Bailey circus.

"I think the cars we designed definitely influenced the styles of the era, but in turn the response of the people also influenced what we designed," said Dave Holls, who retired as General Motors director of design in 1991. "Remember, this was a time when, if you didn't have a car that was fresh enough, new enough, you weren't going to be leading the people. That was the atmosphere of the 1950s. Admittedly, it was certainly naive but that was what led to the creation of so many great cars."

"I started at GM in 1949," said Jordan with a nostalgic lilt in his voice, "and I've got to tell you what automobile design was like. It has always been fun. If

With an investment of $2.19 million, Ford had committed itself to the production of a hardtop convertible. Originally intended for the Mk II Continental, it was finally adapted to fit the new 1957 Fairlane. When engineering did the final tally on the Retractable's design, it had incorporated a total of 522 new parts never before used on a Ford car!

The example pictured is one of the earliest built and is distinguished by the absence of the Skyliner name. Cars assembled during February and March 1957 were shipped to dealers without the Skyliner script affixed to their rear roof panels—an interesting oversight which has made these early production models more desirable to collectors. Interiors were color keyed to the exterior paint scheme.

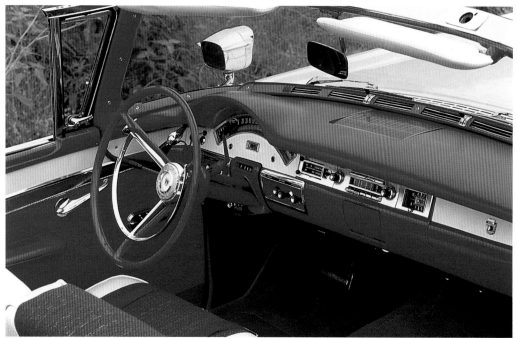

you have a love for automobiles, a passion for them, it never seems like work. It was true back when I was just a young designer, and it was true right up until the day I retired. You go through different eras, you face different problems and you sometimes get out some designs that you're not proud of, but every now and then you get out a design where you say, 'Boy, that's it!'"

Not everyone in Detroit was as delighted with their job as Chuck Jordan. When Semon "Bunkie" Knudsen took over as Pontiac general manager in June 1956, he found himself at the helm of a flagging GM Division in need of a new image. In 1957 and 1958, however, he had to work with what was already on the boards. And, all things considered, what he had wasn't that bad.

Knudsen believed that horsepower and performance were the keys to success and he began his tenure at the Pontiac helm by breaking the "gentlemen's agreement" inspired by Ford and subscribed to by all Automobile Manufacturers' Association (AMA) members, that they would keep their respective companies out of organized racing. Before the year was out, Pontiac was campaigning race-prepped Catalinas. Knudsen even subsidized Smokey Yunick out of his

The Ford Retractable's design required that the roof break and fold in order to fit into the trunk recess. The entire roof came up and then backward into the opened deck, which was operated by its own motors. In the up position, the roof was secured to the body and windshield by a patented system of screw locks. One motor operated each lock in the roof's rear quarters, and a single motor turned both locks in the roof's front flipper by way of two flexible drive shafts. A similar arrangement secured the rear decklid. Interestingly enough, the Ford design was the first patented use of an automated decklid in the industry.

own pocket, just to get the Pontiac name in front of the American public. He also put the lessons learned on the race track to good use beneath the chrome-clad bodies of his production cars.

The 1957 models showed up with the displacement of their V-8 engines increased to 347 cubic inches and horsepower bumped to 270, (up from 317 cubic inches and 227 horsepower). In addition to the standard two-barrel carb and optional four-barrel, the 1957 models could be ordered with Pontiac's new Tri-Power carburetion consisting of a special manifold with three two-barrel carburetors mounted in line. With cylinder heads giving a 10.25:1 compression ratio, Tri-Power equipped engines delivered 321 SAE gross horsepower.

The model which got the most attention and technology in 1957 was the new Bonneville, named after the famous Salt Flats. Ab Jenkins had posted a new 24-hour speed record there in June 1956, averaging 118.337 miles per hour behind the wheel of a stock Pontiac two-door sedan.

The Bonneville was Pontiac's first attempt to design a "niche market" car along the lines of the Chrysler 300 series, a car that would appeal to young, enthusiast buyers. With only a few exceptions, like the sporty 1956 Star Chief convertible, Pontiac still had a stodgy "old man's car" image to overcome.

Initially, the Bonneville was a limited production model available in only one body style, a convertible, powered by a new 370-cubic-inch, 310-horsepower, fuel-injected V-8. A stock Bonneville fuelie could clock 0 to 60 miles per hour in 8.1 seconds and power through the quarter mile in 18 flat. In addition to getting the cars off the line posthaste, the Bonneville's fuel-injection also worked as a fuel saving device, or at least that's the way Pontiac read the 1957 Mobilgas Economy Run results where the cars recorded an impressive average of 20.4 miles per gallon.

On the downside, which may have somehow slipped from memory, we should be reminded that cars built in the 1950s were not designed for performance driving, if that performance veered from a straight line. Their chassis were not engineered to handle sharp curves or transition through esses at breakneck speeds. Their brakes were sorely inadequate and steering virtually devoid of feedback from the pavement. Suspensions wallowed through every dip in the road and cars keeled over like a boat if a driver negotiated a turn too quickly, the result usually being a thrown hubcap. Still, linear performance was better than no performance.

For the 1957 model year, Pontiac produced only 630 fuel-injected Bonnevilles. Admittedly not a great

Every American automaker had its share of marketing disasters in the 1950s—General Motors and Ford, perhaps had more than their fair share. The Cadillac Eldorado Brougham was a financial black hole for GM as was the Continental Mk II for Ford, but the Edsel was perhaps the greatest marketing failure of the decade. Introduced in 1958, the Edsel was more than a new car, it was a new division of Ford Motor Company, just as Continental had been in early 1956. However, unlike the Mk II, which received rave reviews, the Edsel seemed to strike everybody wrong. It was similar to other models from the late 1950s, except for the unusual vertical grille, yet the Edsel seemed to fall from grace almost immediately. After just three years it was discontinued. Oddly enough, Edsels have a very strong following among collectors today.
Automobile Quarterly

number, but the public relations value alone was worth more than individual sales, at least in terms of furthering Pontiac's new image.

For 1958, the Bonneville would become a series with the addition of a new two-door hardtop "Sport Coupe." As Pontiac's new flagship model, the Bonneville was billed as having, "sport car action blended with town car luxury." Built on an expansive 122-inch wheelbase and measuring 211.7 inches (17.6 feet) from bumper to bumper, the Bonnevilles were truly town car sized.

In 1957, Pontiac styling had been tastefully restrained but in 1958, it was no-holds-barred when it came to fixturing the exterior. The 1958s were accented by a new chromed side treatment featuring spear-shaped side moldings with a projectile motif, a sculptured rear quarter panel with four Pontiac stars, four chromed front fender louvers, and stainless steel rocker panel and fender trim. Along with the massive grillework and bumpers, there was enough chrome per car to make every Pontiac owner a quasi-investor in rhodium futures!

Inside, the 1958 Bonneville had a stylish new instrument panel featuring a deep-cove design with a textured aluminum fascia and chromed stand-out instruments.

Pontiac gave Bonneville owners a wide variety of interior and exterior color combinations, which allowed a great deal of personalizing—something sorely lacking from today's new car market. The Bonneville came in Mallard Turquoise, Marlin Turquoise, Deauville Blue, Kashmir Blue, Burma Green, Calypso Green, Redwood Copper, Patina Ivory, and Starmist Silver. And all of these colors could be two-toned in a variety of combinations. Interior upholstery offered four two-tone selections plus the optional leather and Morrokide. In all, there were more than 35 interior and 30 exterior color combinations possible.

The Bonneville's option list included Pontiac's less than successful Ever-Level air ride suspension, Safe-T-Track limited slip differential, Sportable Radio (which could be removed from the dashboard to become an AM portable with its own self-contained battery), and Inside Sliding Sun Visor. This last item—one of the really rare options to find today—was a wide, green plastic shade which came down from the headliner and covered the upper third of the windshield. Pontiac also offered an optional dual exhaust system, power steering, power windows, power brakes, air conditioning, and Memo-Matic 4-Way power seats, which automatically moved back for easier entry and exit when the ignition was off, and then returned to the pre-selected position when the car was started.

The base engine for the Bonneville was the Tempest 395 with Super HydraMatic and four-barrel carburetion. Output was 255 horsepower with 8.6:1 compression, and 285 horsepower with 10:1 compression. There were also two optional engine combinations available: the Tri-Power, 300-horsepower Tempest 395, and the 310-horsepower Fuel-Injected Tempest 395. In 1958, only 400 Bonneville Fuelies were produced. When you look at all the features Pontiac had to offer, it's difficult to understand why the Bonneville didn't sell better. Of the 217,303 Pontiacs purchased in 1958 only 19,599 were Bonnevilles.

In the 1950s, almost every American automaker offered coupes, sedans, station wagons, and convertibles, as complete a range of models as anyone could ask for, but there were those who wanted more. What more could there possibly be? How about a hardtop convertible.

At the turn of the century, when automobiles had only fabric tops, people wanted enclosed passenger compartments. Automakers gave them coupes and sedans. Having done that, there arose a demand for cars with fabric tops. By the 1930s, one could go to a local new car dealer and select either a coupe, sedan, convertible, or phaeton. Some 20 years later, buyers could even have a convertible with an optional removable hard top—Ford offered it on the Thunderbird in 1955, Chevrolet with the Corvette in 1956. Still, you had to choose. You couldn't have a hardtop and a convertible at the same time. Or could you?

The idea of an automobile with a retractable steel roof dates back to the late 1930s, when French automaker Peugeot produced a model that featured a retractable steel top.

In 1948, a proposal for a retractable hardtop design study was ordered by Ford Motor Company. The late Eugene Bordinat, who was a chief stylist at Ford in the 1950s, recounted during an interview in the early 1980s, that when he was in charge of styling they were always looking for ways to make cars more distinctive. Usually that meant adding more chrome embellishments, but a hardtop convertible, said Bordinat, would be a real coup for any automaker who could figure out a practical way to do it.

By 1950, Bordinat, then assistant manager of Ford Styling, had a two-dimensional cardboard model of a retractable hardtop that had been constructed by Ford stylist Gil Spear, manager of Ford's advanced styling studio. The concept gathered steam over the next three years, and in 1953 Ford displayed the *Syrtis*, a 3/8-scale model concept car featuring a futuristic "Roof-O-Matic" convertible hardtop. While only a concept, the retractable hardtop was considered an idea well worth pursuing within Ford. Ironically, designer Jim Huggins, who had worked on the project with Spear in 1950, moved over to Chrysler's Special Projects department a couple of years later, and with him went the idea, if not the actual design.

By the time Ford publicly released photos of the *Syrtis*, Chrysler had already started development of their own hardtop convertible at the Ghia design studio in Turin, Italy. The finished Ghia prototype, called the Dart, was displayed in 1956 as one of Chrysler's futuristic concept cars. A year later it returned with its retractable top removed and a new name, Diablo. If nothing else, word that Chrysler was also at work on the hardtop convertible concept in 1953 had prompted Ford to press on with renewed enthusiasm. With a working scale prototype of the *Syrtis*, the idea was formally proposed to a Ford planning committee, which funded $2 million to develop it as a part of the new Continental Division's product line. In July 1953, the project was officially handed over to John Reinhart, Gordon Buehrig and the Continental design team for final development. The switch from Ford to Lincoln took Bordinat and Spear by surprise, but it did make sense. The hardtop convertible would be both a very costly and a very limited production item. The all-new Continental Mk II was the only model which could be priced high enough to make it profitable.

The Mk II project, under the direction of Reinhart, proposed two models, a two-door coupe and retractable hardtop convertible. There were no plans for a soft top convertible, although two were built, one by Durham for William Clay Ford and another by an independent coachbuilder in Florida.

In order for the Mk II retractable to be completed in time for a 1955 introduction, the design would have to be engineered and tooled in less than 18 months—an almost impossible schedule even for the Detroit of the 1950s, when new models came out almost every year.

Spear's original design, utilizing a track system to lower the top, was abandoned and the Mk II design team came up with a mechanism that would swing the roof back on moving arms, using separate motors to raise the rear deck lid and lower the top. The final design that was adopted by Ford Division for the 1957 Skyliner was based on the Continental design and incorporated 7 reversible motors, 10 relays, 13 switches, 9 circuit breakers and 610 feet of wire!

The design required that the roof break and fold in order to fit into the trunk recess. The entire roof came up and then backward into the opened deck,

The final phase of Chevy's three-year plan culminated with fins and chrome—raising the rear fenders to new heights and accentuating the revised 1957 grillework with Cadillac-inspired bumper guards and a bold Chevrolet bow tie emblem.

Following a styling trend established by Cadillac, the 1957 Chevys sprouted magnificent tailfins, the only year this design was offered.

Mercury had long maintained a reputation as a manufacturer of performance cars, and in 1950, a Mercury convertible, driven by Benson Ford, paced the 34th Indianapolis 500 Mile Race. Seven years later Mercury returned to the brickyard with a history-making, one-year-only new model, the Turnpike Cruiser convertible.

The Turnpike Cruiser was a glitzy car, even for 1957. Mercury produced 1,265 Turnpike Cruiser convertibles, each one an exact duplicate of the pacesetter, painted "Sun Glitter" and fitted with a black Haartz cloth top. The cars were offered with full Pace Car graphics. The car pictured is the actual Indy Pacesetter from 1957, awarded to that year's 500 winner Sam Hanks.

which was operated by its own motors. In the up position the roof was secured to the body and windshield by a patented system of screw locks. One motor operated each lock in the roof's rear quarters and a single motor turned both locks in the roof's front flipper by way of two flexible drive shafts. A similar arrangement secured the rear deck lid. Interestingly enough, the Ford design was the first patented use of an automated deck lid in the industry.

How did the idea end up back at Ford? Given the complexity of the retractable hardtop, it had seemed only logical that it should be offered on a top-of-the-line car. However, as the project reached completion in 1955 and a Mk II retractable prototype was completed, the division's marketing department concluded that given the Continental's limited production run, the retractable could not be built in sufficient numbers to make the car profitable. It was too late to turn back, however. Ford had $2.19 million invested in the design, so it had to go somewhere. The hardtop convertible was up for grabs and Ford Division wanted it back. With some modifications it could be adapted to fit the new 1957 Fairlane, and with greater production numbers a Ford version would be profitable.

The all-new 1957 Fairlane models themselves would have to undergo some major structural alterations to incorporate the retractable system. Building the Skyliner would fast become a game of structural dominos. Each change in design requiring yet

another. A new windshield frame was required to utilize the fastening mechanism. To accommodate the retractable hardtop and its hardware, Ford had to hastily redesign the center and rear floor pan. A recess was needed in the trunk for storage space and the spare tire, otherwise there would be precious little room for luggage when the roof was retracted. In order to create a concealed well for the spare, the fuel tank had to be moved, and it was relocated to a position straddling the driveshaft, just behind the rear seat. Because of the top mechanism and larger decklid, structural support for the rear of the car and trunk area had to be strengthened to minimize body flex. The only drawback to that alteration was that it used up interior space resulting in a nearly vertical rear seat-back. Although this never had any great effect on the car's popularity or sales, it was one of the Skyliner's least desirable traits.

From a distance the Retractable looked almost identical to other 1957 models. Comparing the Skyliner side by side with a 1957 Fairlane, however, the hardtop convertible was some three inches longer in the rear. The roof design also required a blind rear quarter to add strength where the greatest stress would be exerted in the retracting cycle and to conceal much of the operating hardware. The blind rear quarter and more vertical back window were the most recognizable characteristics of the Skyliner. The roof design was almost identical to the Continental prototype's and was divided into two sections, folding one-third of the way back from the windshield. The deck-lid had a folding section that extended to cover the package tray area when the top was lowered. All-in-all, a very complicated design.

In addition to structural changes in the body, the Skyliner also required a special chassis. The frame was 6.12 inches longer than the standard passenger car frame, and 8.56 inches narrower after the 70-inch line. The four-cross member frame incorporated an I-beam X-member to supply additional rigidity to the Skyliner's body. Finally, the new chassis/frame design and completed top mechanism—motors, relays and other bits—raised the car's curb weight, thus requiring brake area to be increased by 191 square inches! The standard six-cylinder engine was also no longer powerful enough to return acceptable performance, so the more expensive Thunderbird V-8 would have to be standard.

By February 21, 1956, and with job one still a year away, nearly all of the details were finalized and Ford's advertising agency, J. Walter Thompson, was given a preview of the 1957 line in order to begin preparation for the year's media campaign. Special emphasis was to be placed on the Fairlane 500 hard-top convertible. Three months later, on May 22, a hand-built prototype rolled onto the Ford test track and the first official photos were taken.

In what appeared to be 11th-hour timing, the final design was approved in December 1956, with the trunk being revised once again to provide a storage bin for small items. The bin was fastened to the floor of the trunk by wing bolts and was located on top of the spare tire compartment. The car was finally ready to go into production. When engineering did the final tally on the Retractable's design, it had incorporated a total of 522 new parts never before used on a Ford car!

What has more than once become an idiosyncrasy within the Ford division, naming the new model had been left to the very end. It happened with the Thunderbird in 1953 and again with the Retractable in 1957. Names had been submitted by J. Walter

Special Pace Car features included a rear decklid ornament, consisting of an illuminated Mercury crest and winged checkered flags. A continental spare was also standard equipment on the Pace Car replicas. Highlighting the Cruiser's distinctive body lines were bold tailfin coves running fully half the length of the car and finished in bright silver.

The engine in the Convertible Cruiser was Mercury's 368-cubic-inch, 290-horsepower V-8, coupled to a Merc-O-Matic transmission with push-button keyboard controls. Power steering and power brakes were standard. At a price of $4,103, the Convertible Cruiser was the most expensive Mercury model in 1957.

Thompson and for the 51A, as the Retractable had been code named, however, none seemed to suit the car and Ford ultimately drew on its own history, selecting Skyliner which had previously been used on the 1954–56 plexiglass-topped passenger car line. One unique roof design gave way to another.

The rest of Ford's 1957 model line was already on sale by September 1956 and the new Skyliner was being touted in the press as a forthcoming model to be released early in 1957. The first cars wouldn't leave the assembly line until February. Meanwhile, the prototype was making the auto show circuit, first in New York, then on to Chicago and Detroit. In April, the first Skyliners arrived in dealer showrooms—and in our living rooms.

Back in the 1950s, for those of us who remember, television offered great theatrical programming—

"The Hallmark Hall of Fame," ABC's "Ford Theater," sponsored by Ford Motor Company, "The Ford Show" on NBC, and "Zane Grey Theater," to name a few. The Skyliner was one of the most publicized automobiles in America. On April 10, 1957, the Retractable made its nationwide television debut during the commercial break on "Ford Theater." It appeared again on April 19 on "Zane Grey Theater" and April 25 on "The Ford Show."

Along with television and radio, the print media was also treated to a full scale blitz. The very first car off the assembly line was delivered to the White House on April 14 and during that same week 1,300 daily and 2,300 weekly newspapers across the country featured the Skyliner in full- and double-page spread advertisements. Unless you didn't own a television, never read a newspaper or

shunned radio, it was impossible not to know about the Ford Skyliner.

Ford's entire 1957 model line was well received and outsold Chevrolet by some 60,000 vehicles for the year. Bordinat had decided to buck the trend in Detroit and simplify the cars with smoother lines and less chrome embellishment. While GM laid on brightwork by the ton, Ford went for subtle enhancement, and let styling make its own statement. For the 1957 model year the Skyliner ranked fourth in overall convertible sales with 20,766 cars sold. First place also went to Ford with 77,728 Fairlane 500 Sunliner convertibles driving off dealer floors. In third place, 21,380 Thunderbirds found their way into American garages. The Chevrolet Bel Air convertible took second place in sales with 47,562 cars, and last in the top five was Pontiac's Star Chief convertible, attracting 12,789 customers.

With Ford convertibles in three out of the top five sales positions, 1957 truly was Dearborn's year to shine. However, despite record sales, the benchmark car for 1957 was not a Ford. It was the Chevrolet Bel Air.

The 1950s, perhaps more than any period since the 1930s, was a decade when automobiles seemed to define the character of the nation, and no automaker did a better job of it than General Motors. Of GM's five divisions, it fell upon Chevrolet to be the standard bearer of the masses—the car most associated with America throughout the 1950s. In fact, no introduction since the Ford Model A signaled a greater shift in the product mentality of U.S. auto consumers than the debut of Chevrolet's 1955 models. Seemingly overnight, Chevy's bold new styling and the availability of a V-8 engine turned the heads of an entire generation that had never before considered buying a

Chevrolet. William E. Fish, Chevrolet's general sales manager at the time, remarked that he had never seen a study that said styling is the one thing that makes people buy, but he added, "We know it's true."

After Chevrolet introduced its redesigned cars—and image—in 1955, body styles were revised annually, giving each model year a distinctive and easily recognizable look. For 1956, Chevy invested a cool million in tooling to give their front fenders "the Cadillac flat look" and lengthen hoods by four inches. A new grille that spanned the full width of the front end and Buick-style taillights completed a very effective restyling effort. In effect, Chevrolet designs, although essentially unique to the division, were an amalgam of GM styling cues taken from Cadillac, Oldsmobile and Buick models. The close resemblance to GM's higher-priced lines was the result of extensive deliberation and by no means coincidental. The Chevy Bel Air was often referred to as "the baby Cadillac."

The final phase of Chevy's three year 1955–1957 design cycle culminated with fins and chrome—raising the rear fenders to new heights and accentuating the revised 1957 grillework with Cadillac-inspired bumper guards and a bold Chevrolet bow tie emblem. The 1957s also gained a sportier stance with the use of 14-inch wheels, leading to a slight reduction in overall height.

It didn't take many words to sum up the source of Chevrolet's newfound popularity. Introducing the 265-cubic-inch V-8 in 1955 marked the beginning of a new era, elevating Chevy from the ranks of the relatively unexciting to one of the hottest cars on the American road. By the end of the 1955 model year there were 1,646,681 proud new Chevrolet owners.

The 1957 and 1958 Eldorado Biarritz were the last rear-wheel-drive models to have exclusive body styling. Some collectors believe they will ultimately become a more desirable car than the 1959 due to less ostentatious styling and more exclusive production numbers.

The interior of the 1957 and 1958 Cadillac Eldorado Biarritz was one of the most lavishly appointed in Cadillac's postwar history. A large steering wheel framed a wide and heavily chromed instrument panel on the driver's side, while the front seat passenger faced equally bright dashboard trim containing the radio. Following a styling trend that began with the 1953 Eldorado, the dashboard's brightwork wrapped around into the door panels.

The 1956 models burst on the scene with a grandiose display of performance at Pikes Peak. A pre-production Bel Air driven by Zora Arkus-Duntov shattered a 21-year record by making the 12.42 mile ascent in 17 minutes, 24.05 seconds (the previous record was 19 minutes, 25.70 seconds). The road up Pikes Peak climbed through 170 sharp turns and cutbacks to the summit, 14,110 feet above sea level, and had not only been a good test of the car's suspension and handling, but had proven the power and acceleration capabilities of the 265 V-8.

"The Hot One's Even Hotter" was the tag line in 1956 advertising, and by year's end it proved to be more than just a sales pitch. Chevrolet closed the books on 1956 ahead of arch rival Ford for the second year in a row and in the number one sales position in the country; 26 percent of all American cars sold in 1956 were Chevrolets. In an analysis of the American automotive industry, *Fortune* magazine estimated that if Chevrolet split off from General Motors, its sales volume would still rank either fifth or sixth among all American corporations, ahead of DuPont and Bethlehem Steel and not far behind General Electric.

Chevrolet had saved the best for last, rolling out its styling and performance *pièce de résistance* for 1957. The only way Chevrolet could improve upon the previous year was to come out with an even more powerful V-8—and that's exactly what they did. When the restyled 1957s hit dealer showroom floors, buyers were offered a choice of seven different V-8s with outputs ranging from 162 horsepower all the way up to a whopping 283 horsepower. At the top of

the option list was GM's brand new 283-cubic-inch, 283 horsepower fuel-injected V-8 with a 10.5:1 compression ratio. The 1957 fuelie was nothing short of a production line hot rod. With one brake horsepower per cubic inch, Chevy advertising touted, "The Road isn't Built that can Make it Breathe Hard!" Coupled with a new optional Turboglide automatic transmission, offering a built-in "kickdown" feature, 1957 fuelies had almost unrivaled passing power.

As history will attest, the 283 Chevys passed just about every car built in the 1950s, becoming not only the most popular model of its time, but also one of the most prized collector cars ever built.

By the 1950s, greater media coverage of the Indianapolis 500 had convinced automakers that there was a significant publicity advantage in sponsoring the pace car for the annual Memorial Day race. Mercury had long maintained a reputation as a manufacturer of performance cars, and in 1950, a Mercury convertible, driven by Benson Ford, had paced the 34th Indianapolis 500. Seven years later Mercury returned to the brickyard with a history-making new model, produced for just one year, the Turnpike Cruiser convertible. (This is not to be confused with the Mercury Montclair Turnpike Cruiser convertible, built in 1958, which was similar in appearance but very limited in production.)

The Turnpike Cruiser was a glitzy car, even by 1957 standards. Following the lead established by Dodge in 1954, Mercury produced 1,265 Turnpike Cruiser convertibles, each one an exact duplicate of the Indy 500 pacesetter.

The Cruisers were painted "Sun Glitter" and fitted with a black Haartz cloth top. Other special features included front fender turn indicators and a rear decklid ornament, consisting of an illuminated Mercury crest and winged checkered flags. A continental spare was also standard equipment on the pace car replicas.

The Cruiser's interior featured all vinyl crushed grain two-tone upholstery in "Sun Glitter" yellow and black. On the extreme right of the dash, each of the cars had a silver plaque stating that it was a true replica of the 1957 Indianapolis pace car. At a price of $4,103, the Convertible Cruiser was the most expensive Mercury model in 1957. Due to their popularity, the "1,265 Club" was later formed for owners of 1957 Turnpike Cruiser Pace Cars. Today, roughly 106 of the original cars have been accounted for, and except for the 1954 Dodge Royal 500, it is the rarest of 1950's Indy pace car replicas.

It seems odd to look back at the 1950s from a 1990s viewpoint. Here we are in an age of unprecedented technology, automated assembly lines, computer aided body design and engineering, and yet it takes up to five years to design a new car. Back in the 1950s, a period dominated by manual assembly lines

and artist-conceived body designs, Detroit managed a new model almost every year. Of course, back then cars were easier to build; there were no government regulations, no emissions standards, in fact there was nothing to prevent automakers from doing whatever they wanted. And what they wanted most was to make last year's car seem obsolete.

At Ford's luxury division, the 1957 model year came on the heels of a successful 1956 season which had narrowed the sales gap between Lincoln and Cadillac. Most of the news for 1957 centered around the Lincoln Premiere and lower-priced Capri models.

While a long-awaited four-door hardtop was added to the lineup in 1957, the most significant styling change for Lincoln was the introduction of tailfins and quad headlights. The term "quad," as applied to the 1957 Lincoln's new Quadra-Lites, was something of a misnomer—they were not true duals. The upper unit was a separate headlight with low and high beam, while the bottom was an auxiliary driving or road light, controlled by an independent dash switch. In 1956, the road lights had been located below the bumper and the move up in 1957 was simply to give the impression of the more avant-garde dual headlight designs on Cadillacs and several other American makes.

At the rear, larger and more daringly canted tailfins

The 1957 Eldorado Brougham was the most expensive American car built in 1957. Only 400 were built that year and another 304 in 1958. Cadillac's response to the Continental, the Brougham drew much of its exterior styling from GM's Orleans Motorama show car. The pillarless four-door concept was a favorite of Harley Earl, as was his design for the stainless steel top, a feature that would become an Eldorado trademark.

The Cadillac Fleetwood Sixty Special was one of the most physically imposing American automobiles of the 1950s. This 1958 model fitted with the dealer-installed continental spare was nearly 20 feet in length.

rose upward from redesigned fenders, accented by flared quarter-panels and chromed "false" airscoops beginning just behind the front doors. While providing the 1957 Lincolns with a noticeably updated appearance—in other words tailfins—to keep pace with the latest Detroit styling trend, the changes were neither costly nor difficult to accomplish. The rear bumpers were also changed for 1957, as much for styling as for practicality. In 1956, the exhaust tips had stylishly exited through cutouts in the bumper. While being quite clever, the design proved itself unpopular with owners who watched the chrome on their bumpers discolor in short order. For 1957, Lincoln wisely redirected the tail pipes below the bumper, filling the former exhaust openings with back-up lights.

The 1957 Lincolns boasted a number of new and improved features and accessories, such as power vent windows, electric door locks and a new six-way power seat. Another new feature was a padded dashboard in place of the original vinyl-covered metal dash used on 1956 Capris and Premieres.

A "Direct-Power" differential (Lincoln's version of Positraction) was available for 1957 along with optional Adjust-O-Matic shock absorbers. Power steering and brakes were standard equipment on all Lincoln models, while under the hood, a slightly revised 368-cubic-inch V-8 developed a whopping 300 horsepower—good enough to propel the 4,362 pound Premiere to 60 mph in 11.5 seconds. Pretty heady stuff for a family car in 1957!

The Capri and Premiere rode on a full-length, boxed-siderail frame with four crossmembers and an "X" member for added rigidity. Both Lincoln models shared the same 126-inch wheelbase and stretched 224.6 inches (roughly 18.7 feet) from chrome bumper to chrome bumper.

To provide the Premiere and Capri with responsive handling, yet retain a comfortable luxury car ride, Lincoln used a ball-joint-type independent front suspension with improved telescopic-type Hydro-cushion shock absorbers and a torsional stabilizer bar. In the rear, the live axle relied on long-leaf type springs with eight leaves, tension-type shackles which adjusted spring stiffness to road conditions and telescopic shock absorbers. Rounding out the Lincoln's underpinnings were four-wheel hydraulic brakes with large 12-inch drums surrounded by 8.20x15 white sidewalls.

With 300 horsepower, the optional "Direct-Power" differential and a very solid suspension, the 1957 Premiere offered drivers spirited performance, good cornering and a better than average ride. *Motor Trend* summed up the Premiere in its November 1956 preview as a model which "need not take a back seat to any car as one of America's top luxury automobiles."

The "top luxury automobile" *Motor Trend* was referring to was, of course, Cadillac. Just as Lincoln had

Fins, fins, fins. Every year from 1955 to 1959 they grew in size and height, and Cadillac's grew the most. The 1957 models (top) had modest fins that shot up to dagger tip dorsals in 1958 (center). The all-new 1959 models (bottom) took the tailfin to its maximum height, parking the taillights almost at other drivers' eye level.
Cadillac Division

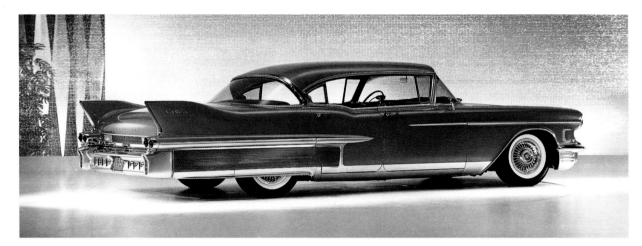

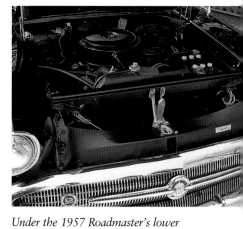

Under the 1957 Roadmaster's lower profile hood was a powerful 300-horsepower V-8 engine equipped with a four-barrel carburetor and handily able to launch a four-door Roadmaster from a stand to 60 miles per hour in 10.6 seconds with a top speed of around 120 miles per hour! For a full-size family car, these were very impressive figures. With a 10:1 compression ratio, the 364-cubic-inch engine developed a hefty 400 foot pounds of torque at 3,200 rpm. Compared with the previous year's models, the 1957 Century, Super, and Roadmaster had 17 percent more horsepower.

All 1957 Buicks, like this Roadmaster 75, featured dramatically lowered body lines. Buick referred to the design as a "Low-Sweep silhouette," a shape which better harmonized with the stylish wraparound windshields and backlights introduced by General Motors in 1954. On average, 1957 Buicks measured three inches lower at the roofline and were over three inches longer than in 1956.

made headway with the 1956 Premiere and introduction of the Continental Mk II, Cadillac had also set about creating a new luxury standard.

Cadillac's 1956 model year had been highlighted by three benchmarks. First, Cadillac production topped 150,000 for the first time ever. The Eldorado was renamed the Eldorado Biarritz and a new companion model, the Eldorado Seville two-door Hardtop Coupe was introduced.

A fresh look came with the restyled 1957 Eldorados, the most luxurious and fashionable models yet to bear the name. Along with the bold new exterior appearance of the entire 1957 line, the Biarritz Convertible and Seville Hardtop Coupe were treated to their own exclusive decklid, bumper and tailfin design, this time a softly rounded deck and fender combination with dagger-tipped fins.

The Biarritz and Seville were also joined by a third model in 1957, the Eldorado Brougham. Virtually hand-built, only 400 were produced in 1957 and 304 in 1958. The Brougham was Cadillac's response to the Continental, nothing short of a passion play for Cadillac which spent more money building the cars

than they could sell them for! If it was just to make a point, it was well taken. The Eldorado Brougham was the most luxurious automobile of the 1950s.

The Brougham drew much of its exterior styling from GM's Orleans Motorama show car. The pillarless four-door concept was a favorite of Harley Earl, as was his design for the stainless steel top, a feature that would become an Eldorado trademark.

The body styling was totally new for Cadillac in 1957 and the Brougham was built on a wheelbase measuring only 126 inches. A touch over 18 feet in overall length, it was shorter than any other Cadillac sedan, just 55.5 inches high but a cavernous 78.5 inches wide.

The novelty of power accessories was still new and the Brougham had them all—power windows, power door locks, even power vent windows. The trunk opened and closed electronically—requiring three motors to operate—even the starter was automatic, only requiring the driver to turn the key to the ON position. The front seats were power with preset adjustments to automatically change the seat back angle, seat height and distance from the steering wheel for two different drivers. More than enough to

ABOVE AND RIGHT
The Century was built on a 122-inch wheelbase. For 1957 the Series 60 Century and Series 40 Special were the only models to use a real three-piece rear window.

impress even the most jaded car buyer in 1957. But Cadillac went further.

Each car came equipped with a Vanity Set that included a silver comb and mirror, lipstick holder, tissue dispenser and four silver drinking cups in the glove box, along with a compact and powder puff for the ladies and cigarette pack holder for the gents. In the rear seat center arm rest was a compartment which held an Arpege atomizer with Lanvin perfume, a mirror and a leather notebook finished to match the car's upholstery.

In 1959, the Eldorado Brougham was completely redesigned and the bodywork contracted out to Pininfarina in Turin, Italy. A total of 99 were built.

The Cadillac V-8 was very much a part of the Eldorado image, and the Biarritz and Seville were powered by either the standard 365-cubic-inch, 300-horsepower V-8 or an optional 325-horsepower engine, equipped with dual four-barrel carburetors and teamed with Cadillac's three-speed Jet-a-way automatic transmission. The 325-horsepower V-8 was standard on the Brougham.

The Eldorado line remained basically unchanged in 1958, as General Motors observed its 50th anniversary. Among the characteristics distinguishing the

1957 and 1958 Biarritz and Seville models, was the switch to quad headlights, with four 5 3/4-inch sealed beams replacing the two 7-inch units used the previous year. The quad headlamps were actually introduced in 1957 as an exclusive feature of the Eldorado Brougham. The 1958 Eldorado's lower rear body panels were further embellished with 10 vertical chrome strips, and new emblems were used on the tailfin and trunk lid.

Under the hood, the Biarritz gained in horsepower once again, with the addition of a third two-barrel carb, Cadillac's version of Tri-Power, giving the 365-cubic-inch V-8 an output of 335 horsepower.

The 1958 Eldorados would be the last rear wheel drive Cadillacs to have totally distinctive styling all their own. Production of the convertible totaled a mere 815 in 1958, second only in limited numbers to the Eldorado's introduction in 1953.

For 1959, Cadillac surprised everyone with yet another completely redesigned one-year-only model line. This would represent the most opulent statement in chrome and fins ever—the height of the tailfin, both figuratively and in terms of popularity. Not only was the Eldorado Biarritz an exercise in outrageous

excesses, but so was the entire 1959 model line. Every Cadillac had massive chrome-edged fins rearing up from just behind the doors, sweeping skyward and dissected midway by twin bullet taillight lenses virtually at eye level to most other cars. They were so large that drivers often mistook their own tailfins for another vehicle in the rear view mirror!

Only 1,320 of the high-finned 1959 Eldorados were built, selling for a base price of $7,401. The Eldorado closed out the 1950s as the flashiest American car of the era.

In 1957, Edward T. Ragsdale, GM vice-president and Buick general manager, proclaimed Buick's all-new model line "a new way of motoring." While that remark may have suffered from an overdose of corporate enthusiasm, the 1957 Buicks were virtually brand new from the wheels up.

Buick offered a total of four series. The Series 40 Special was available in seven body styles: a Convertible, two- and four-door Riviera, Estate Wagon, Riviera Estate Wagon, and two- and four-door Sedan. The Series 50 Super line was made up of three models: two- and four-door Rivieras, and a convertible. The Series 60 Century line had a convertible model, two- and four-door Rivieras and the Caballero Estate Wagon. The top of the line Buick was the Roadmaster Series 70, offering both two- and four-door Rivieras and a convertible.

Behind the Century's gleaming brightwork was Buick's high-performance B-12000 V-8. The vertical-valve V-8 worked at a 10:1 compression ratio producing 300 horsepower and 400 foot pounds of torque. Quadrajet carburetion delivered fuel to the 364-cubic-inch engine and quick response to the throttle.

In its *1957 Facts Book*, Buick wrote: "The Century—true to its tradition—is the most competitive car of the year. Century power is now 50% higher than the 1954 model that brought this great Buick back into the market with such spectacular performance that the trade promptly began referring to it as 'the banker's hot rod.'"

Of all the models that had been available from Buick in 1957, the Century was the fastest. It had the big 364-cubic-inch engine, the same one used in the Roadmaster, but the Century was built on a shorter and lighter 122-inch wheelbase. (The Series 40 also shared the same platform, while the Series 50 and 70 rode on a 127 1/2-inch frame). The Century measured 208.4 inches in overall length, half a foot shorter than the Roadmaster.

The 1957 models featured dramatically lowered body lines. Buick referred to the design as a "Low-Sweep silhouette," a shape which better harmonized with the stylish wraparound windshields and backlights introduced by General Motors in 1954.

On the average, 1957 Buicks measured three inches lower at the roofline and were over three inches longer than in 1956. Drawing more attention to the rear of the car, tailfins and chrome became dominant design elements particularly in the size and visual impact of the front and rear bumpers.

Under the Buick's lower profile hood was a new and more powerful 300-horsepower V-8 engine equipped with a four-barrel carburetor and handily able to launch a four-door Roadmaster from a stand to 60 miles per hour in 10.6 seconds and a top speed of 120 miles per hour.

For a full-size family car, these were very impressive figures. To accomplish this performance, GM engineers had made some rather extensive changes to the basic Buick V-8 engine first introduced in 1953. Displacement grew from 322 to 364 cubic inches through a 0.0125-inch increase in bore and a 0.2-inch increase in stroke. To accommodate the longer stroke, the height of the cylinder banks had been raised 0.25 inches and the connecting rods lengthened 0.1 inches. While these changes might not have been considered major on most engines, the Buick V-8 was already so compact that the increase in stroke required changing the design of the block.

Other engine improvements for 1957 included larger intake and exhaust valves, extractor-type exhaust manifolds, and four-barrel carburetion. With a 10:1 compression ratio, the 364-cubic-inch engine developed its 300-horsepower output at 4,600 rpm, and a hefty 400 foot pounds of torque at 3,200 rpm. Compared with the previous year's models, the 1957 Century, Super, and Roadmaster had 17 percent more horsepower. They also had poorer fuel economy, but that wasn't exactly a big concern in the 1950s when a gallon of gasoline cost less than today's morning paper, but the question of miles per gallon was nevertheless raised at a Buick press conference, to which Ragsdale replied off the cuff, "Well, we have to keep the gas companies happy." Just imagine what the media would do with that remark today!

The 1957 Buicks offered more than a new body and an improved engine. What couldn't be seen in the car's trim, 58-inch high roofline, or experienced with an exhilarating application of the driver's right foot, could be felt in the way the 1957 Buicks rode. The engineering staff had created a hybrid chassis for 1957. To achieve the lower body height, the frame side rails were flared out between the front and rear wheels, allowing the floor pan to be positioned below the rail tops—what GM designers called a "step-down" principle. A new ball joint front suspension was introduced, which included Buick's "anti-brake-dive" front end geometry. (Chevrolet had offered it first in 1955.)

In contrast to some of this seemingly new technology, the rear suspension consisted of a traditional semi-floating axle, supported by coil springs and braced from excessive sway by a radius rod. Buick also continued to rely on torque tube drive. Engineers felt that the superior torque absorption of the tube drive

was an important feature of the Buick ride.

Also improved for 1957 was Buick's Dynaflow transmission. The new "Twin-Turbine Variable Pitch Dynaflow" automatic offered smoother shifts and a more responsive throttle. From a standing start the Dynaflow delivered quicker acceleration, though as *Motor Trend* pointed out in its February 1957 road test, it wasn't necessary to floor it in order to get maximum performance. The *MT* staff made a point of hinting at excessive throttle as the main culprit for the V-8's poorer gas mileage. "If you use the 'take-your-time' method," wrote Pete Molson, "you may later be amazed at the large difference in your gas mileage." Of course, human nature being what it is, few Buick owners had eggs poised between the sole of their shoe and the ribbing of the accelerator pedal. They punched it. The car went faster and so did the fuel. Oh, well.

Overall, the 1957 Buicks were everything Ragsdale had said they were—and more. The automotive press found the entire Buick line to be improved in almost every respect, especially handling and steering response. Ideally, the all-new model line for 1957 should have had customers flocking to Buick showrooms, assuring Buick's lock on the number three position in new car sales, but that was not the case. Although superlatives for the new models sprouted like violets in April, the American public was less than

The 1957 Buick Century interiors offered a wide color combination of nylon and Cordaveen fabrics. The Rivieras were upholstered in either black with ivory, rust with ivory, green, or blue.

enthusiastic and did some serious pruning of Buick sales. By year's end, GM's number two luxury car division had slipped into fourth place with annual sales totaling only 407,283—an appreciable drop from the previous year's 572,024. For 1958, Buick tried an end run around the competition by introducing the gaudiest cars in the company's history which helped the marque settle into fifth place with a mere 257,124 sales.

In an effort to bolster flagging sales, Buick introduced a new model in March 1957—the Roadmaster 75—a custom-built car described by Buick in one word: Magnificent.

Basically a fully equipped Roadmaster, *everything* was standard on the 75—six-way power seats, power windows, power steering and WonderBar radio. The only option was air conditioning. Inside the Roadmaster 75 luxury upgrades abounded: combination leather and broadcloth upholstery, padded carpeting, carpeted lower door panels and leather-trimmed door caps were standard features, and the entire dashboard was one broad, chromed grin from door to door. In addition to all of these features, the 75 also offered one mechanical advancement not available on any other Buick model until 1958—finned aluminum front brake drums.

As Buick's flagship, the 75 was priced at only $126 less than a Cadillac Series 62. There were subtle similarities between the top-line Buick and Cadillac models for 1957, which GM hoped would reinforce Buick's position as the luxury car line right below Cadillac. The Super four-door Riviera, Roadmaster Riviera and 75 all shared their roofline, wraparound windshield and sail panel rear door design with the new 1957 Cadillac Sedan de Ville, Fleetwood Sixty Special and Series 62 four-door hardtop.

The Roadmaster 75 was the ultimate expression of Buick luxury and elegance in 1957, as close as Buick buyers could come to owning a well-equipped Cadillac.

Throughout the late 1950s Detroit's styling studios took everything to the extreme, and the new car showroom became a battleground upon which American car makers fought the war of chrome and fins. While most people consider the 1959 Eldorado to be the most outrageous car of the era, the most pretentious set of wheels to roll down an American road in the late 1950s belonged to the 1958 Buick Century Caballero Estate Wagon.

Had National Lampoon's *Vacation* been filmed back in 1958, the Caballero could easily have taken the place of Clark Griswald's Wagon Queen Family Truckster. No other line of cars built in the 1950s had as much chrome trim as the 1958 Buicks, considered today by some automotive historians to be the ugliest cars ever produced by GM. But, beauty is in the eye of the beholder . . . .

The Caballero embodied every styling cliché that Detroit designers had conceived since chrome and fins crawled out of the post World War II primordial ooze. The 1958 Buick's massive Fashion-Aire Dynastar Grille opened up like a lascivious grin, with 160 chromed squares, each of them with four triangular surfaces to reflect light, bordered by chromed bullet parking lights on either end, and a Cadillac-style lower bumper supporting two large conical grille guards.

Having decided to try and overwhelm the public with gingerbread in 1958, Buick's chrome obsession continued with new Vista Vision dual headlamps and chrome-edged brows that continued down the side of the car into a bold sweepspear leading to the rear wheel openings, and then rising up over the wheel arches back to the bumper, capped at either end by massive chromed bumper guards. Heaven help any car that was backed into by a 1958 Buick!

Not to be outdone by the bumpers, the rear quarter panels were accented with gaudy chromed louvers and ten speedlines tracing back to tall, chrome draped tailfins. It's no wonder the Caballero weighed in at more than 4,500 pounds.

The 1958 Buicks did have their finer points, however, with very stylish cut down front doors, and on two- and four-door hardtop models, a pillarless window arch that gave the cars a stunning profile.

Styling gaffs alone did not footnote the 1958 model year. Buick suffered the fate of several GM Divisions with the introduction of an optional air suspension system, Buick's having been dubbed "Air-Poise Suspension." "Air Poison" might have been more appropriate. Problems with the new design helped kill off Buick sales in 1958, contributing to the GM Division's fall to fifth place in the industry.

Similar to Cadillac's air suspension system, which also proved faulty, Buick's was comprised of four rubber bellows filled with compressed air. A high-pressure tank, fed from a compressor run by the engine, was mounted on the car's frame. The air in the bellows was to be kept at 100 psi, counteracting roll and sway on curves or crowned roads. Each bellows was composed of a chamber consisting of a metal container, into which a rubber diaphragm was compressed by means of a plunger connected to the suspension. An added feature was a lift, actuated by a lever under the instrument panel. It permitted the driver to raise the car body up to 5.5 inches and was intended primarily for use in tire changing, getting out of deep mud or snow, or when a high curb interfered with opening the doors.

Buick advertising claimed that regardless of the load, the car would be kept at a constant level at all times. It just wasn't so. Like the air suspensions used on other GM models, the idea looked great on paper but fell well short of expectations in practice. The chambers leaked overnight and owners often found their cars resting mere inches off the ground in the morning

While most people consider the 1959 Eldorado to be the most outrageous car of the era, the most pretentious set of wheels to roll down an American road in the late 1950s belonged to the 1958 Buick Century Caballero Estate Wagon. The entire line of Buick Estate Wagons shared a 122-inch wheelbase chassis. At the top was the Model 69 Caballero, equipped with the 300-horsepower V-8. Next in line was the Model 49D Riviera, with a 250-horsepower engine, and last the lower-priced Model 49 Estate Wagon.

Caballero's interior choices were distinctively patterned grain Cordaveen in two-tone green, two-tone blue, red and white, black and white, tan and beige, plus a rust cloth with beige bolsters. As a safety feature, padded dashboards upholstered in matching Cordaveen were available. Adding to the Estate Wagon's versatility was a divided rear seat option that folded down in 1/3 or 2/3 sections. As a hauler, with the rear seats down, the wagon offered a 101.9-inch platform with a total load space of 64.5 cubic feet.

(on the road the pressure would pump up again), and on the highway, the air suspension tended to react violently to bumps and dips. At their best, the 1958 Buicks were clumsy beasts. Plungers on curves and rippled surfaces, they leaned like a sailboat tacking into the wind, and overall, were a real handful to control. Fortunately, there was Dynaflow. Or perhaps not.

For 1958, which marked the 10th anniversary of Dynaflow, Buick introduced its new Flight Pitch Dynaflow, another less than wonderful idea. Three turbines instead of two were used to increase torque output. In theory, the concept was very good, but it was too complicated to manufacture reliably. Problems notwithstanding, Buick went ahead. GM engineer Joe Turlay, who worked as director on the triple turbine project, remarked some years later that the Flight Pitch design had some pretty strange performance characteristics. "A stop watch told you it was doing fine, but your sensibilities told you [inaccurately] that it was slipping like a son of a bitch." Ultimately, it proved to be too expensive. Buick invested $86 million in tooling for the triple turbine Dynaflow, only to scrap it a few years later.

On the positive side, Buick offered the best brakes in the business for 1958, with the adoption of air-cooled aluminum front brake drums with a radial fin design and cast iron linings for faster cooling of the

friction surfaces. Expanded to the entire Buick line, the new brake design had been introduced the previous year exclusively on the Buick Roadmaster 75.

As for Buick's transgressions in chrome, they only occurred in the 1958 model year. The 1957s had been more tastefully trimmed, offering a straightforward evolution of the '56 look, and the 1959 model year brought forth a totally new generation of Buick models and body designs. The 1958s, however, are the most interesting to look at. Buick only produced 4,456 Century Caballero Estate Wagons. They were the last of their kind, a historic high water mark in outrageous styling.

Have you ever wondered how a mere automobile, an amalgam of metals, fabrics, rubber and castings can defeat the passage of time and become highly coveted years after its introduction? It happens often but not to every car. To become collectable a car must have a unique aura, something that grabs your attention, stirs the imagination, keeps you awake at night, or perhaps causes your thoughts to stray during the day. These are the seeds of avarice that render artifacts desirable and turn otherwise sensible people into collectors.

Virgil Exner no doubt had this in mind when he created the Chrysler 300C; however, it's doubtful that he planned for its popularity to last for over four decades.

Like so many Exner designs from the 1950s, the 300C was the end result of styling experiments that had taken form through a variety of concepts, what Exner liked to call "Idea Cars." Throughout the 1950s, Exner's influence on Chrysler styling was equal to that of Harley Earl's at General Motors. Like the GM Motorama cars, Exner's Idea Cars at Chrysler helped to set design standards automakers both here and abroad would follow for more than a decade. The 1957 Chrysler model line may have been the zenith of that trend.

Chrysler's 1957 models caught GM, Ford, and the rest of the automotive industry completely off guard with dramatic new styling proffered as the "Forward Look." Indeed, the 1957 Chryslers bore no resemblance to their predecessors, or for that matter, any other cars on the road. The greatest benefactor of that change, however, was the 300C.

The origins of the 300C can be found in a series of Virgil Exner Idea Cars dating back to 1952. The first was the Chrysler Special, built in Italy by Carrozzeria Ghia. In 1953, Exner had two additional cars built by Ghia, the Thomas Special and Chrysler d'Elegance. All three examples shared a similarity with bold trapezoidal grilles and sweptback bodylines. The Ghia Falcon and Chrysler "613" (300C prototype), both completed in 1955, gave rise to the final evolution of Exner's front end styling for the 300C. The wedge-shaped bodylines and lofty tailfins were adapted from a pair of 1955 Idea Cars known as Fire-Sweep I and Fire-Sweep II, designed by Chrysler stylist Maury Baldwin. Combining Exner's "613" design, the Fire-Sweep concept cars shown at auto shows throughout 1955 and 1956, accurately forecasted the look of the all-new 1957 300C.

The third series Chrysler Letter Car made its debut on December 8, 1956, at the New York Auto Show. From any angle, this was a car unlike any that had been offered by an American automaker. From the massive Ghia-inspired grille, consuming most of the front end, to the dynamic wedge shaped body culminating in tailfins, that for 1957 reached an unparalleled high, the 300C was more of a sensation than any competitive model offered by GM or Ford. Truly unrivaled for 1957, the 300C was destined to become the best selling of all Milestone Letter Cars.

Behind the massive 300C grille, Chrysler's standard engine for 1957 was a 392-cubic-inch, 375-horsepower, Fire Power V-8 with special hardware, including mechanical tappets, stronger push rods, adjustable rocker arms, double valve springs, valve seat inserts, twin four-barrel intake manifold, and carburetion, dual air cleaners, lighter-weight valves, hardened crankshaft, tri-metal bearings, high-output camshaft, special piston rings, custom calibrated distributor, high-temperature spark plugs, and speed-limiting radiator fan.

For those desiring something more, an optional 390-horsepower engine-and-chassis package priced at

$550 provided a more radical camshaft, 10.0:1 compression; limited-slip differential; 2.5-inch low back pressure exhaust system; heavy-duty clutch and driveshaft; manual transmission; manual steering; and a choice of 13 different axle ratios that allowed performance to be tailored to any conditions of use. Although this package was primarily for professional racers, more than a few ended up on the street.

The 300C was offered with two transmission choices, the three-speed TorqueFlite automatic as standard equipment and a three-speed manual gearbox as part of the chassis-and-engine option package. The automatic had push-button controls on the dashboard and the governor on the unit was recalibrated for the higher torque output of the 392-cubic-inch engine. On the 18 cars built with stick-shift, a 1957 Windsor steering wheel was used, a cover was placed over the push button control housing and the power steering, power brakes and air conditioning features were deleted.

Still built on the New Yorker's 126-inch wheelbase, the 300C was only one-half inch longer than the original Chrysler 300. Its air-duct brake-cooling system and new torsion-bar suspension were among the most important technical innovations in the industry for 1957. Torsionaire-Ride was hailed as a revolutionary system with torsion-bar front springs and ball-joint wheel suspension. Briggs Cunningham had used

With a base price of $3,487, the Caballero's option list included air conditioning and the Wonder Bar Radio, which could be tuned to preselected stations by push buttons, scanned for a station with the auto push bar, or operated by the driver from a floor-mounted switch. Power windows were available along with six-way power seats. Loaded with all of Buick's available options for 1958, the Century Estate Wagon, at more than 17 feet in length, provides all the conveniences of home, and nearly as much square footage!

Adventurer interiors featured luxurious, color-keyed, pale gold cloth with a metallic gold and white vinyl trim combination. The standard safety dash pad was covered in a contrasting shade of gray, with matching gray tone floor carpeting.

a similar setup on his 1953 Le Mans machinery and all Chryslers got it for 1957. The 300's system was special with 40 percent stiffer bars to provide the race car type of ride. In combination with several other factors, like revised front-end geometry and a low center of gravity, the Torsionaire feature produced the best road handling in America at the time.

The all-new 300C had some big shoes to fill on the performance side. In 1956 the 300B had become the champion of American stock car racing with 37 AAA and NASCAR titles, and an Unlimited Stock Class victory at Daytona. Although factory sponsored racing was on the decline by 1957, due to the competition ban instituted by the AMA, driver Red Byron captured first place at the Daytona Safety and Performance Trials with a new 300C, recording a top speed in the Flying Mile of 134.128 miles per hour. Granted, the 300C wasn't quite as fast as the lighter, record-setting 300B driven to a two-way record of 139.9 miles per hour by Tim Flock in 1956, but it was better looking by a wide margin and still the only full-size, six-passenger American car capable of cruising at 100 miles per hour.

For 1957 Chrysler offered five exterior finishes with a tan leather interior standard. A handful of cars were ordered with interior combinations not officially listed as options. These units received an "888" code designation which signified a nonstandard upholstery selection, rather than a specific color choice. Such cars are exceptional rarities today.

Compared to any other car offered by an American automaker in 1957, the Chrysler 300C was in a class by itself, and a pretty limited class at that. Total production of the 300C coupe was just 1,918.

While Exner's 1957 Chryslers fired the first volley in the battle of chrome and fins, Ford and GM answered in 1957, 1958 and 1959, to close out the decade with the wildest American cars of any era in automotive history.

Confusion. Where would automotive history be without it? Historically speaking, confusion is the foundation for research, finding out all the details—who designed the car, who engineered it, what options were available, how many did they build, and occasionally, the almost unanswerable question, why did they build them at all?

For DeSoto, the question of "why" is the real historical imperative. As it turns out, the marque was Walter P. Chrysler's answer to Dodge, which the Chrysler Corporation did not own when approval was given to design a companion car line priced between the all-new Plymouth and Chrysler models. There is some conjecture that Chrysler developed the DeSoto as a competitor to Dodge merely to intimidate the New York banking house of Dillon, Read & Company, which had purchased Dodge in 1925, into selling out, which in fact they did, in 1928. However, by the time Dodge fell into the Chrysler fold, the DeSoto was already on the assembly line, and a new American marque was about to be born.

When the all-new DeSoto line was introduced in 1928, the company established a first-year sales record delivering 81,065 cars in 12 months—a record that would stand unsurpassed until 1960, when Ford introduced the new Falcon. Ironically, 1960 would also be the final year for DeSoto production.

The decision to discontinue a model line is seldom an abrupt one, and the handwriting was most likely on the corporate wall when the 1958 DeSotos were introduced.

Making its first public appearance at the Chicago Auto Show on January 5, 1958, the limited production Chrysler DeSoto "Adventurer" offered the ultimate in DeSoto engineering and styling, combined with the characteristic Flight Sweep design of the three standard DeSoto series—Firesweep, Firedome, and Fireflight—introduced in fall 1957.

Although the Adventurer looked remarkably similar to the rest of the 1958 model line, with its Virgil Exner-designed, high-canted tailfins and "Signal Tower" taillights, the cars were based on the companion Chrysler 300 Series, with the DeSoto Adventurer displaying its own distinctive exterior colors and trim.

Following the basic design theme of all 1958 models, the Adventurer featured a flared area on the rear quarter panel, accented by a finely textured triangular insert of anodized aluminum, with the name "Adventurer" appearing in gold script.

Adventurer interiors featured luxurious color-keyed pale gold cloth with a metallic gold and white vinyl trim combination. The standard safety dash pad was covered in a contrasting shade of gray, with matching tone floor carpeting.

Distinctively styled Adventurer wheel covers, with a new center spinner, were standard, as were the upper rear deck chrome strips, which won popularity on the 1957 Adventurer. The aluminum mesh grille, gold-anodized for protection in all types of weather, also provided an additional individual touch.

The 1958 Adventurer was equipped with DeSoto's new Turboflash V-8, displacing 361 cubic inches with a 4.125x3.375-inch bore and stroke and deep-breathing compression ratio of 10.25:1. The Adventurer engines included a high-performance camshaft, new valve springs with surge dampers on both intake and exhaust valves, new intake manifold, dual four-barrel carburetors, dual-point distributor, a hefty output of 345 horsepower at 5,000 rpm, and a tire-chirping 400 foot pounds of torque at 3,600 rpm. DeSoto also offered an optional fuel-injection system boosting horsepower to 355 at 5,000 rpm.

In previous years, DeSoto's limited production models had virtually sold out before the first cars ever came off the assembly line. For 1958, the limited edition Adventurers were available in two models, a two-door hardtop and a convertible. Rare by any standards, only 82 Adventurer convertibles were built, and only 11 are known to exist today.

"There is not a fiercer hell than the failure in a great object," wrote John Keats. In 1959, Chevrolet found out exactly what he meant.

In 1957, GM's major models featured all-new bodies but next to Exner's Dodge, DeSoto, and Chrysler designs its efforts appeared less than inspired. Even Cadillac's striking new Eldorado Biarritz paled in comparison to Chrysler's dazzling 300C convertible. For Chrysler's crosstown rivals, the gauntlet had been thrown down and with Harley Earl retiring in 1958, it was picked up by an army of his disciples.

In a period of less than two years, GM's styling departments tried to redesign all five automotive lines, and this Herculean effort strained GM's resources to the limit. The results, some say, were the ugliest cars ever produced, the majority of which are considered highly collectable today.

The country was in love with the automobile, madly in love with GM. And then that love betrayed them in 1959. Perhaps betrayal is too harsh a word, misled would be more accurate. But who misled whom? One of Ford's chief stylists in the 1950s was Eugene Bordinat. He commented on the era some 30 years later, "Most cars designed in the 1950s were created to appease the consumer, more than follow the dictates of good taste. We were pandering to the public," declared Bordinat. "From an aesthetic standpoint it was tasteless, but I won't make any apologies for what we did back then. It was 'in' for the day, the public thought it was great, and we sold one hell of a lot of cars."

At Chevrolet, everything seemed to be falling into place for chief stylist Claire MacKichan, until photographs of the 1959 models reached the desk of Chevrolet boss Ed Cole. Cole began to wonder if GM had stepped too far ahead of public tastes and quickly dispatched 1959 Chevrolets on a series of public showings.

The limited production Chrysler DeSoto Adventurer offered the ultimate in DeSoto engineering and styling, combined with the characteristic Flight Sweep design of the three standard DeSoto series—Firesweep, Firedome, and Fireflight—introduced in the fall 1957.

The comments that came back weren't encouraging.

In Dearborn, photos of the 1959 Chevys caught the attention of Ford Division's new chief Robert McNamara, a rank and file conservative who had already made a name for himself by killing off the two-passenger Thunderbird. McNamara had opted to follow a relatively traditional path for 1959 and feared that Chevrolet's flamboyant horizontal tailfins, huge rear windows and exotic front end design would trounce Ford's middle-of-the-road styling. As it turned out, his fears were unwarranted. Whereas Ford would later boast about the Gold Medal for Exceptional Styling that it had won at the 1959 Brussels World's Fair, Chevrolet's 1959 models would be the target of cartoonists like Charles Addams, whose famous *New Yorker* lampoon pictured a small boy running from the family garage crying, "Mama, something's eating my bicycle!"

The 1959 Chevy's conference-table-sized deck-lid, 32-cubic-foot trunk, and batwing fins prompted *Mechanix Illustrated*'s bombastic road tester Tom McCahill to claim it provided enough space "to land a Piper Cub."

Before the new models were even unveiled, GM brass could see the writing on the wall. The horizontal fins and huge rear window, combined with a very busy grille and enough chrome to make driving toward the sun hazardous to oncoming traffic, were just too much. With an 80.8-inch width, 119-inch wheelbase, and 210.9-inch overall length, the 1959s looked out of proportion. The one saving grace was the Impala convertible.

With the massive roofline and huge backlight gone, the car was toned down enough to make the horizontal tailfins seem credible. Actually, pretty cool looking by 1950s standards.

Beneath the new body, Chevrolet had done yeoman work on engineering improvements for 1959, including 11-inch drum brakes, a stiffened X-frame chassis featuring an added rear cross-member, and a revamped rear suspension layout incorporating a new anti-sway bar. Transmission choices totaled seven with three three-speed manuals, two Powerglide automatics, a Turboglide auto and a sporty Borg-Warner four-speed with floor shifter—the latter a first for Chevrolet passenger cars.

Standard engines were a 135-horsepower six-cylinder and a 283-cubic-inch 185-horsepower small-block V-8. Neither were really suited to the size and weight of the car. Options included a 230-horsepower, 283-cubic-inch four-barrel and two extremely rare Ram-Jet fuel-injected 283s, rated at 250 and 290 horses, respectively. Chevy's Rochester fuel-injection system made its last appearance as a passenger car option during the 1959 model year.

At the top of the engine list were the 348-cubic-inch big-blocks. Introduced in 1958, the 348 "W-head" V-8 was initially designed with truck duty in

Chevrolet boss Ed Cole began to wonder if GM had stepped too far ahead of public tastes with the 1959 Chevy's huge rear deck and flat tailfins. The one saving grace was the Impala convertible. With the massive roofline and huge backlight gone, the car was toned down enough to make the horizontal tailfins seem credible.

Whereas Ford would later boast about the Gold Medal for Exceptional Styling that it had won at the 1959 Brussels World's Fair, the 1959 Chevrolet's conference-table-sized decklid, 32-cubic-foot trunk, and bat wing fins would prompt writers like Mechanix Illustrated's bombastic road tester Tom McCahill to claim it was "big enough to land a Piper Cub."

mind, but quickly made the transition to passenger car service once a need for more torque was recognized. For the heavy Chevys of 1959 an engine built for a truck wasn't too far off target. All 348s had relatively high compression, 9.5:1 or better, relied on at least a four-barrel carburetor and sported dual exhausts. The ultimate 348 offered during the engine's four-year run, 1958 to 1961, was the Special Super Turbo Thrust, which was fed by three Rochester two-barrel carburetors and used solid lifters in place of the tamer Turbo Thrust's hydraulic units.

Author Mike Mueller sorted out some of the confusion over the 348's horsepower figures and availability in the September 1992 issue of *Car Collector* magazine. Wrote Mueller: "Initially in 1958, the four-barrel Turbo Thrust 348 was rated at 250 horsepower, while the tri-carb Super Turbo Thrust produced 280 horses. At the top was another Super Turbo Thrust V-8 not necessarily meant for the street. Featuring a Duntov solid-lifter cam, 11:1 compression and various beefed components, this race-bred mill pumped out 315 horsepower. In 1959, the same lineup apparently carried over, with a 300-horsepower Special Turbo Thrust 348 four-barrel joining the ranks.

"About midyear, the 315-horsepower Super Turbo Thrust was replaced by an even more powerful 335-horsepower Special Super Turbo Thrust version featuring streamlined exhaust headers and 11.25:1 compression. Some sources rate this engine at 345 horsepower, and others list 305- and 320-horse versions, numbers which were advertised prominently on the hoods of NASCAR stockers. More confusion was added when engineers added better heads with bigger

ports and valves, creating the 350-horsepower Special Super Turbo Thrust tri-carb V-8 for 1960. Some claim that this high-strung, high-powered factory race engine first appeared in 1959. Either way, under the hood of a 1960 Chevy, the 350-horsepower package was capable of high 13s at more than 100 miles per hour in the quarter-mile."

When the 1959s started arriving at dealers, the traditional barrage of customers anxious to "trade up" suddenly became hesitant. This was the third "brand new" Chevy in as many years and one that had already been barbed by the press and run over by the competition. From introduction day, Chevrolet waged a showroom battle against Ford, offering incentives to help move the 1959 models. Ultimately the cars from Dearborn edged out Chevrolet with a final tally of 1,468,451 Fords to 1,416,076 Chevrolets. Ironically, six years later, Chevrolet's general sales manager Lawrence Averill noted that while the 1959 model had not been a great seller when new, it eventually became a sought-after used car!

Despite all the criticism it received in 1959, the Chevy Impala was far from being the most grandiloquent car on the American road. That honor still belongs to the Cadillac Eldorado, closely followed by the Buick Century Caballero station wagon and Buick Electra, a rolling greenhouse with more window glass than a five-and-dime. In fact, compared to most GM cars built in 1959, the Impala was a pretty attractive set of wheels.

When 1960 rolled around, tailfins were in decline, chrome was in remission and America was on the threshold of a new era in automobile design. But that's another story.

A stark contrast to the 1959 models, the 1958 Chevy Impala was a relatively sedate design that might have been better left alone for another model year.

THE
BIG THREE'S
COMPANY

CHAPTER **6**

When GM, Ford, and Chrysler Were Not Alone

Failure. That's a word no one likes to hear, yet throughout the automobile's history in America there have been far more failures than successes. The ratio is better than 100 to one.

Today we have General Motors, which accounts for five original U.S. makes—Cadillac, Buick, Oldsmobile, Pontiac, and Chevrolet (discounting GMC trucks, Saturn, and Geo); Ford with a total of three—Ford, Lincoln, and Mercury; and then Chrysler bearing four brand names—Chrysler, Plymouth, Dodge, and Jeep. Of the latter, Chrysler inherited Jeep when it absorbed American Motors in the late 1980s, bringing us to the topic of lost marques—those companies which are no longer with us.

In the 1950s, the U.S. automotive industry was comprised not only of Ford, GM, and Chrysler (which at the time also consisted of DeSoto) but also of Packard, Hudson, Studebaker, Kaiser-Frazer, Nash, and Willys, among major manufacturers.

Packard, Studebaker, and Hudson were the top three independents and Hudson was among the most prominent American marques to survive into the postwar 1950s. While most people remember Hudsons built in the 1950s, they forget that Hudson was one of America's oldest automakers, producing their first car in 1910.

From the very beginning, Hudson was known for performance. In April 1916, a Hudson set a one-mile straightaway stock car speed record of 102.5 miles per hour at Daytona Beach. In May, at Sheepshead Bay, the 24-hour stock car record was taken at a 74.8 mile per hour average, a mark that would go unbroken for 15 years. And it was a Hudson that set the world's first double transcontinental record, driving from San Francisco to New York and back in September 1916.

It was no surprise to those who knew Hudson's history that the Hudson Hornet burst upon the postwar automotive scene and found almost immediate celebrity in AAA and NASCAR racing. From 1951 through 1954, Hudson Hornets won more stock car races and more season

No shortage of chrome on the Hornet. Instruments were almost blinding. The dashboard was color keyed to the exterior of the car. This 1953 model is equipped with the optional Dual-Range Hydra-Matic Drive transmission.

The Hudson Hornet Hollywood Hardtop was one of the most dynamic models in the 1953 lineup. Only 910 were built that year.

All Hornets were powered by the H-145 308-cubic-inch, inline six-cylinder, side-valve engine. The engines featured an exclusive chrome-alloy cylinder block and "Power Dome" aluminum cylinder head. Output was a substantial 145 brake horsepower at 3,800 rpm. In 1954, the bore was increased from 3 13/16 to 3 15/16 inches (stroke remained the same at 4 1/2) and compression was upped from 7.2:1 to 7.5:1. As a result, horsepower rose to a vigorous 160 at 3,800 rpm. In the hands of skilled tuners, the Hornet's 308-cubic-inch L-head six could be urged to deliver up to 210 brake horsepower for competition. The Twin-H was an option from 1952 through 1954. Twin Carter carburetors gave the stock 308 a boost to 160 brake horsepower.

The Hollywood had that certain sense of style all hardtops of the era displayed. "Large streamlined window areas," said Hudson sales literature, "give you a sweeping view of all outdoors. Trim posts are slim and out of the driver's line of view." Indeed, the wraparound rear window and narrow C-pillars practically gave the driver a panoramic view.

Hudson-built cars challenged and beat Detroit's big guns in NASCAR competition from 1951 through 1954. Hornets won more stock car races and more AAA and NASCAR season championships than GM, Ford, or Chrysler and accomplished this amazing feat wielding a 210-brake-horsepower, 308-cubic-inch, L-head six-cylinder engine against the Big Three's latest V-8s. Automobile Quarterly

championships under AAA and NASCAR auspices than any other American make. And mind you, this was accomplished with an inline six-cylinder engine competing against the best V-8s GM, Ford and Chrysler had to offer!

In the hands of skilled tuners, the Hornet's 308-cubic-inch L-head six could be urged to deliver up to 210 brake horsepower. Hudson also offered factory support through "severe-usage" options designed for racing applications. Hornets had responsive handling, quick steering, and an almost unbreakable suspension. Driver Tim Flock became the 1952 NASCAR champion behind the wheel of a Hornet Club Coupe, and in 1953, Marshall Teague's Hornet won 12 of 13 AAA stock car events. Drivers Herb Thomas, Dick Rathmann, Sam Hanks, Frank Mundy, and Al Keller drove Hudson Hornets to a staggering 65 NASCAR victories. In all, Hudsons had won more than 125 AAA and NASCAR events by 1954. A Hornet even finished sixth overall in the 1951 Carrera Panamericana, well ahead of any other "stock" cars in the Mexican road race, and behind only by two Ferraris and three highly modified American cars competing in the open-modified class.

Victory in showroom stock, of course, did not always guarantee showroom sales, and by late 1953 Hudson was facing the reality of a declining market share and the probability of a merger with Nash in order to survive.

But even as Hudson's star was dimming, the company still managed to produce one of its truly bright spots: the Hornet. Introduced in 1951, Hornet models were offered in four different body styles: a four-door Sedan, two-door Club Coupe (a favorite for racing), two-door Convertible Brougham, and the sleek, two-door Hollywood Hardtop.

Of the four, the convertible was the most attractive, but the Hollywood had that certain sense of style all hardtops of the era portrayed, a kind of subtle convertible-at-heart sportiness. "Large streamlined window areas," said Hudson sales literature, "give you a sweeping view of all outdoors. Trim posts are slim and out of the driver's line of view." Indeed, the wraparound rear window and narrow C-pillars practically gave the driver a panoramic view. And the Hollywood's "Hudson-Aire Hardtop Styling" came at a $3,095 price—competitive to sedan and coupe models.

All Hudsons featured an exclusive "step-down" chassis design that placed the passenger compartment within the frame members, allowing a lower overall height for the car, just 60 3/8 inches, and a lower roofline, without sacrificing headroom. For the early 1950s, Hudsons were considered among the safest cars on the American road, at least for passengers. Because of the "step-down" design, Hudsons also had a lower center of gravity, and thus were less likely to roll over. The passenger compartment was surrounded on all sides by the base frame, and steel girders extended outside the rear wheels to provide greater protection in the event of a collision.

Proven in competition for three years, the entire Hornet line offered exceptional handling and cornering capability with an A-arm and coil spring independent front suspension and rugged solid axle rear with semi-elliptical leaf springs. Further contributing to the Hornet's road holding reputation were direct-acting shock

Nash had been scaling down automobile dimensions since the early 1950s, far ahead of the demand for compacts which would arise in the coming decades. In March 1954, Nash introduced the tiny Metropolitan, built in England by Austin and Fisher-Ludlow, to Nash specifications. With an 85-inch wheelbase, the Model 541s were among the smallest automobiles ever sold in the United States. On April 9, 1956, American Motors announced the new Metropolitan 1500, available in both convertible and hardtop versions. Metropolitans were originally powered by a 42-horsepower Austin engine. The new 1500 increased output to 52 horsepower. The Metropolitan was sold in the United States and Canada from 1954 to 1956 with deliveries in the period totaling 94,986.
Automobile Quarterly

Nash models like this 1951 Rambler Custom Airflyte convertible were popular but not strong enough to keep Nash an independent company as the 1950s wore on. Nash and Hudson merged to form American Motors and the Nash name was eventually dropped in place of Rambler.

absorbers at all four corners, a dual-acting front stabilizer, and a lateral stabilizer in the rear. Combined with its low center of gravity and "Center-Point Steering" system, the Hudson was very likely the best handling and best built American car in its price class. Still, showroom sales did not reflect a level of consumer enthusiasm commensurate with the car's features, or reviews of the day. Pioneer car tester Tom McCahill proclaimed the Hornet as "one of America's finest cars," in 1951. "Its comfort, quality and performance are hard to beat at any price. If you like 'em big, fast, and tough," wrote McCahill, "the 1951 Hornet is your car."

The Hornets measured out at 208 inches from bumper to bumper (over 17 feet) on a 124-inch wheelbase and tipped the scales at 3,600 pounds. All four models were powered by a 308-cubic-inch, inline six cylinder side valve engine, drawing fuel from a Carter two-barrel carburetor. The Twin-H option (twin carburetors) was available from 1952 through 1954 and boosted the stock 308 to 160 brake horsepower. A manual transmission with column shift was standard, and a dual-range HydraMatic available as an option.

From 1951 through 1953, output from the L-head six with the single Carter was a substantial 145 horsepower at 3,800 rpm. In 1954, the bore was increased from 3 13/16 to 3 15/16 inches, (stroke remained the same at 4 1/2 inches) and compression was upped from 7.2:1 to 7.5:1. As a result, horse-power was raised to a vigorous 160 at 3,800 rpm (170 brake horsepower with Twin-H). A nice way to go out. These were to be the last high performance engines to emerge from Hudson as an independent automaker.

On May 1, 1954, Hudson officially became part of the new American Motors Corporation, a merger between Hudson and Nash that was to set the stage for an even larger merger between the new American Motors Corporation and Studebaker-Packard. On May 27, Hudson employees were notified that production was being moved to the Nash automobile factory in Kenosha, Wisconsin. When the 1954 Model run ended at Hudson's Jefferson Avenue plant in Detroit on October 30, 1954, so did an era in automotive history. The 1955 Hudsons were restyled Nash models, and all that remained of the great Hornets and the Hollywood Hardtop was a name.

The merger with Nash was a survival move, not only for Hudson but Nash as well. During the 1930s, Nash had held a steady place in American car production and in 1937 merged with the Kelvinator Corporation, the well-known maker of refrigerators. This came about because company founder Charles Nash wanted George Mason as his executive vice president and to get Mason he had to buy Kelvinator. Mason was no stranger to the auto business, having been with Studebaker, Dodge, and Chrysler before becoming

At the introduction of the bullet-nosed Studebaker, Chief Stylist Raymond Loewy said, "We aimed for the light, fast impression of an airplane. If we could give our cars a feeling of motion and speed, we'd have succeeded in going directly against the current trend. What better way was there to do it than to peel the car away from the front of the hood? The car now cuts its way through the air like an airplane." Tucker designer Alex Tremulis said that the designs and patents were purchased by a lawyer named Jay Darlington after Tucker was liquidated. When the 1950 Studebakers were introduced Darlington sued Studebaker for patent infringement on the design of the spinner nose. Of course, on the Tucker it had been a headlight not a grille, and as a result the court ruled that similarity was not a patent infringement. This was a great relief to Ford which used a similar design on its 1950 models.

president of Kelvinator in 1928. With Mason's arrival, Nash felt he could begin to slow down and at age 74 went into semi-retirement, leaving the operation of Nash-Kelvinator to Mason.

Nash started the 1950s in excellent financial shape and was one of the first American automakers back in production in 1945, winning third place in sales behind Ford and Chevrolet. Of course, once the Big Three got rolling, Nash quickly tumbled back to 11th place. Even so, profits were high and the company recorded an $18 million profit in 1947.

When Charlie Nash passed away in 1948, at the age of 84, Mason moved up the corporate ladder and appointed as his right-hand man, George Romney (in later years Michigan's governor and a presidential candidate). Under Mason, Nash broke new ground in several areas, including the importation of cars built jointly by Nash, British automaker Donald Healey, and Italian coachbuilder Battista "Pinin" Farina. The larger Nashs had also been styled by Pinin Farina, giv-

ing the American cars a more European flavor.

Mason's general philosophy was to offer buyers automobiles that the big-three Detroit establishment did not, and in 1950 he broke new ground with the Rambler, a compact car built on a short, 100-inch wheelbase and powered by an economical 85 brake horsepower six-cylinder engine.

Despite an interesting product line, Nash soon found itself in the same shape as other independent automakers who were rapidly losing market share to GM, Ford, and Chrysler. By early 1953 the market share of the independent car makers had declined from 18.6 percent in 1946 to less than 5 percent.

Mason reasoned that if you can't beat 'em, join 'em. He formulated a plan wherein Nash would merge with Hudson, at the time the biggest merger in the American automotive industry, and Packard, under the direction of Mason's friend James Nance, would acquire Studebaker. The final merger would combine all four companies, giving American Motors

The 1950 Studebaker's wraparound rear window gave the driver excellent rear visibility and passengers an open view of the scenery.

The redesigned 1952 Studebaker Commander convertible was chosen as the Official Pace Car for the Indianapolis 500, giving Studebaker the added visibility it needed to entice customers into the showroom. Author collection

Built on a 120-inch wheelbase, the 1955 Studebaker President hardtop coupe was the sportiest model in the lineup except for the Speedster. Powered by Studebaker's 175-horsepower Wildcat ohv V-8, the President could accelerate from 0 to 60 miles per hour in just 13.4 seconds and run the quarter mile in 18.1.

and Studebaker-Packard a market share almost equal to the Big Three. It was a plan that might have worked had Mason not died in October 1954 just five months after the Nash-Hudson merger. Romney, who had no interest in merging American Motors with Studebaker-Packard dismissed the plan as a fool's errand.

In the late 1940s and early 1950s, Studebaker had been a force to be reckoned with. Innovative and highly competitive, the South Bend, Indiana, company brought in the best engineers and designers available to create the first all-new postwar models sold in the United States.

At Studebaker's design helm was internationally renowned stylist Raymond Loewy, and a staff headed by Virgil Exner, Gordon Buehrig and John Reinhart.

Loewy's first postwar design, introduced in 1946, gave way to an all new model in 1950 with a controversial look that to this day is still the subject of debate. It was either one of the most innovative designs of the era or one of the ugliest.

After Reinhart and Buehrig moved on to Ford and Exner to Chrysler, Loewy set about designing American cars with a European look. The 1953 Studebakers were stunning. The automotive press heaped superlatives on the new models, comparing them in importance with the first Lincoln Continental and the Cord 810. General Motors, Ford and Chrysler may have been bigger but for this one brief moment in history the little company from Indiana was stealing all the press and giving Detroit something to think about.

Unfortunately, against Detroit's big guns, Studebaker

could not build a competitively priced car. Studebakers were too expensive and the company's way of doing business left dealers with no margin to price their cars competitively. With what amounted to the best cars Studebaker had built in years and perhaps the best American cars of the early 1950s, Studebaker found itself facing a legion of disgruntled dealers and ledger pages scored in red ink.

Into this best-and-worst-of-times scenario came the 1955 models, introduced on the heels of Studebaker's merger with Packard. It was the beginning of the end for both companies.

The 1955 Studebaker line consisted of 10 six-cylinder Champion models, 10 Commander V-8 styles, and five Studebaker Presidents, the Deluxe sedan, State sedan, State coupe, State hardtop, and Speedster hardtop.

Built on a 120-inch wheelbase, the President hardtop coupe was the sportiest model except for the Speedster. The coupe was powered by Studebaker's 175-horsepower Wildcat ohv V-8. The Studebaker President could accelerate from 0 to 60 in just 13.4 seconds and run the quarter mile in 18.1 at a speed of 79.8 miles per hour.

The styling for the coupe, first introduced in 1953, was pure Loewy, as distinct from any other car on the road as Loewy was from any other designer. Whatever his shortcomings, he was a master at selecting the best works of others and blending them into a single composition. It was Loewy's condition that the designs of everyone working for him automatically became his which prompted Exner, Reinhart, and Buehrig to leave. Loewy's design team for the 1953 models was headed by stylists Bob Bourke and Bob Koto. The original design was actually for an auto show special, however, unlike many concept cars which were experimental, Loewy based his design on the probability of going into actual production. Faced with a choice between following the styles set by Detroit in the early '50s or striking out in a new direction, Loewy and Studebaker chose the latter, going with a low, sleek, European silhouette for 1953.

The Loewy models broke new ground with the lowest height in the industry, just 56 inches to the roofline. The one-piece wraparound rear window was another first, adding to the car's unique visual appeal. A low, nose-down grille and fender contour gave the Studebaker models an aggressive appearance unlike any American car on the road. There was no mistaking a new Studebaker.

As were the trends of the time, more chrome was required with each successive model year and the 1955 Studebakers brought forth new front end and body side trim designs to rival anything shining brightly from Detroit.

Sadly, Studebaker had only two models which could command the respect of critics and buyers alike,

Studebaker interiors were not overly ornate. Loewy chose simple themes that were easy on the eye and not slathered with chrome trim, as were so many Detroit designs of the era.

A low, nose-down grille and fender contour gave the Studebaker models an aggressive appearance unlike any American car on the road in the 1950s.

OPPOSITE
The styling for the Studebaker coupe, first introduced in 1953, was pure Loewy. The cars broke new ground with the lowest height in the industry: just 56 inches to the roofline. The one-piece wraparound rear window was another first, adding to the car's unique visual appeal.

the coupe and speedster. Loewy's sporty styling did not translate well to the Studebaker sedans and station wagons. The coupes were in short supply while the rest of the model line sat languishing on dealer lots. Compounding the problem, Studebaker prices were the highest in the industry compared with competitive Ford, GM, and Chrysler models. Studebaker was a company on the brink of failure.

If we speak here only in terms of aesthetic success and not financial, if we disregard the ledger sheets, corporate problems, manufacturing delays and poor management, the Loewy-designed Studebaker coupes, as an individual product, were a great success. The right cars, at the right time, for the wrong company.

Packard was not in much better shape than Studebaker. Although financially sound, sales were abysmal compared to the prewar era when buyers of prestige automobiles regarded Packard as the equal of Cadillac and Lincoln. The stylish Packard Clipper's

re-launch in 1946 was meager with only 42,102 cars produced for the 1946 and early 1947 model years.

Packard introduced its all-new 1948 Twenty-Second Series in mid 1947. While it is hard to believe that any design could prove unpopular in the car-starved postwar 1940s, Packard's Twenty-Second Series was less than revered. The same can be said of the 1949–1950 Twenty-Third Series, a mildly facelifted carry over of the previous model line.

Since Packard did not follow the trend of introducing new models at the same time of year as other automakers, there was often an overlap and when the 1950 model year ended, the sales figure tally of 106,457 Twenty-Third Series cars included only 42,640 sold as 1950 models. A dismal performance at best.

Packard management had diluted the model line in an attempt to offer lower-priced models competitive with Ford, GM, and Chrysler's low-priced leaders. The all-new Twenty-Fourth Series, introduced in 1950 as a 1951 model, improved the calendar year

ABOVE AND OPPOSITE
The star of Packard's all-new 1953 model line was the stunning Caribbean. The limited-production convertible was designed by Dick Teague and based on Richard Arbib's 1952 Pan American show car which was built for Packard by the Henney Motor Company of Freeport, Illinois.

but by then Packard had lost much ground to the competition and in the eyes of luxury car buyers, tarnished its prestigious image.

The once imperious Packard empire was teetering on the edge when James J. Nance was elected president and general manager in 1952. He had inherited both the postwar problems, which were the obvious, and others as yet unseen.

By 1953, Nance had begun an overhaul of Packard which appeared to be working by mid year, and then he began to run afoul of unforeseen problems at almost every turn. During the first quarter, Nance's marketing strategies brought Packard the best sales

period in its history. A revamped 1953 model line, headed by designer Dick Teague's beautifully styled Caribbean and the reintroduction of the Packard Clipper name, brought customers back into dealer showrooms. By 1954, Nance had upgraded the Packard line with more luxurious and expensive models to compete with Cadillac and Lincoln, and expanded the Clipper series to compete against lower-priced models from GM and Chrysler. Poised for a Packard renaissance in 1955, everything around Nance began to crumble.

The undermining of the Packard empire had begun in December 1953, when Briggs, Packard's principal coachbuilder, sold out to Chrysler. Consequently, Packard had to

create its own in-house facility to manufacture bodies. In 1954, Nance concluded the merger of Packard with Studebaker, the first phase of a planned conglomerate that would include Nash and Hudson. When the merger with American Motors fell through, Nance was saddled with the financially challenged Studebaker company which was losing money faster than Packard could make it up.

The final blow to Nance's plans followed a decision to relocate the Packard assembly line in the former Briggs building on Conner Avenue. The refitting of the plant was ill-conceived, rushed to completion and fraught with problems that could not be corrected before the next generation Packards went into production. Cars were coming off the line with such poor quality that dealers had to make repairs before they could sell them. In the face of unprecedented warranty repairs, Packard posted a loss of $30 million in 1955. Compounding this loss, earlier, Studebaker-Packard

Packard went out with a great line of cars in 1956. The redesigned Caribbean was offered in both convertible and hardtop versions, the latter being extremely rare.

had lost a $426 million government defense contract to General Motors, a contract that Nance had been banking on.

Despite such adversity, the new Packard models were beautifully styled cars loaded with features including Packard's own automatic transmission and a superb suspension system that rivaled the best from GM, Ford, or Chrysler. These were achievements that should have been impossible given Packard's problems, but this was Nance at his best, under fire. Back in 1952 when he had been hired to run the company, he told Packard stockholders at the annual meeting, "Make no little plans, they lack the magic to stir men's souls." By 1955, however, Nance's magic was quickly vanishing. He had the wisdom and foresight of Walter P. Chrysler but the luck of Preston Tucker.

The 1955 Packards introduced the company's first V-8 engines, available in either 327- or 352-cubic-inch displacements, a revised dual-range automatic transmission, and new Torsion Level suspension, the best in the industry. *Motor Trend*'s review of the 1955 models said, "Everything else dims by comparison with ride . . ." *Car Life* proclaimed Torsion Level as ". . . a great contribution to the world's motoring industry. Not only is the 1955 Packard safer than many of its contemporaries, but it is much more comfortable." Floyd Clymer Books, which published a variety of automotive and general interest publications, applauded the car's ability to go into a turn at speed, with the body remaining almost perfectly level. So what went wrong? Conner Avenue.

The handsome 1956 Packard 400 was the end of the line. It was a car incorporating the best features Packard stylists and engineers had put into a single design, but one that buyers were skeptical of due to problems with the 1955 models. Public confidence in Packard had been shaken to its very roots. The failure of the 1956 models led to the resignation of President and General Manager James Nance on July 25, 1956, the same day Packard automobile production was suspended in Detroit. Production was moved to Studebaker's South Bend, Indiana, plant but for all practical purposes, Packard was through.

Packard incorporated the latest engineering advances in its 1956 models, including the Twin Ultramatic transmission, designed by Forest McFarland and his associate, former Chrysler engineer, John Z. DeLorean. The Ultramatic used a pushbutton gear selector mounted off the steering column.

The Packard 400 brought down the curtain on Packard as an independent automaker. Declining sales and stiff competition from GM, Ford, and Chrysler finally forced Packard into a merger with Studebaker, an alliance that ultimately led to the failure of both companies.

Author Richard Langworth called Kaiser-Frazer the last onslaught on Detroit. Indeed, few had the financial resources or the willingness to take on the Detroit establishment. After World War II, the demand for new cars was so great, that Kaiser and partner Joseph Frazer ventured where few had dared to go since the 1930s. In 1946, they introduced the first Kaiser-Frazer automobiles. K-F set up shop in the Willow Run plant built by Henry Ford to produce Liberator bombers during the war. The first K-F models, designed by Howard Dutch Darrin were remarkably handsome. K-F went from nonexistent to number eight in new car sales in just two years selling a total of 325,806 cars in calendar years 1947 and 1948. Automobile Quarterly

By 1949, when K-F restyled their model lines, GM, Ford, and Chrysler had introduced all-new postwar models as well, cutting deeply into K-F sales which fell to 57, 995, putting K-F in 17th position. Models produced throughout the early 1950s ranged from the 1951 Henry J compact (a contemporary of the Nash Metropolitan) to the large Kaiser Dragon (pictured) and Manhattan, along with the sporty Kaiser-Darrin 161 sports car. Offering as complete a range of cars as possible, but selling too few to keep the business profitable, Kaiser finally ceased operation in the United States. Kaiser did continue to produce cars and Jeeps in Buenos Aires, Argentina, through Industrias Kaiser Argentina SA (IKA). This gave the Kaiser design another seven years of life. Automobile Quarterly

The plant was so ill prepared for mass production that it took until late 1955 to get all the bugs worked out and by then it was time to retool for 1956. Nance, ever the optimist, kicked off the annual meeting with the slogan, "Nothing can stop us now!" In truth, it should have been, "We have met the enemy, and he is us."

Better than half a century of Packard automobile production, a reputation second to none and a great piece of American automotive history were on the road to extinction. The 1956 models were the best Packards in more than a decade but it was too late. The buying public had lost confidence. Packard, which had intended to save Studebaker, was now at the mercy of that very company. On July 25, 1956, the same day James J. Nance resigned, it was announced that Packard production would be moved to Studebaker's South Bend, Indiana, headquarters. The 1957 models were slightly made-over Studebakers, and Packard as an individual marque ceased to exist.

By the end of the 1950s, all of the independent automakers had either gone out of business or merged into larger companies. General Motors was king, Ford and Chrysler the heirs apparent and American Motors a niche manufacturer that would continue to build interesting but not always successful automobiles for another 25 years. Gone from the American road were such respected names as Packard, Hudson, Nash, and DeSoto. Gone, but not forgotten.

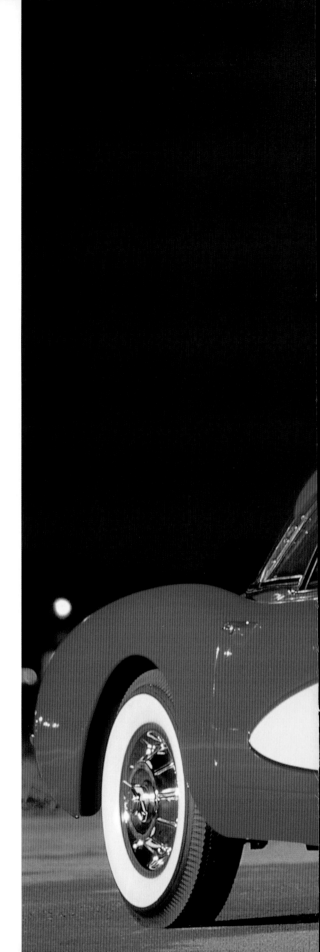

THE SPORTS CAR WARS

CHAPTER 7

Corvette, Thunderbird, Crosley, and Darrin

Americans had never been high on sports cars prior to the late 1940s. This was perhaps due to the fact that the idea was very European. Certainly there were "sporting" American cars, Cadillac, Packard, Lincoln, even Duesenberg offered speedsters, but they were nothing like the competition-bent designs of prewar Jaguars, Bugattis, and Alfas, cars built for a purpose very few Americans cared to indulge in—amateur sports car racing. Those who did purchased cars abroad and had them shipped home. They were few, however, and their sway on the automotive industry little felt. The American ideal of a sports car had yet to be realized.

It wasn't until the late 1940s that Americans began to experience firsthand the joys of driving small two-seaters like the MG TC. By 1952 there were 7,449 MGs registered in the United States and it had become the best-selling imported sports car in America. The little cars from Morris Garage had pried open the door and what drove through next was the Jaguar XK120, a road car that could be just as easily raced as driven to the country club.

The sports car as we know it today was really defined by racing. From the late 1930s forward, the shape of cars built for competition established the path automotive stylists would follow for decades. Jaguar founder and chief designer William Lyons was no exception and his XK120 was the car that had the greatest influence on Harley Earl's design for the 1953 Corvette and Frank Hershey's design for the 1955 Thunderbird.

During the early 1950s, New York auto importer Max Hoffman was introducing to America's automotive elite the 356 Porsche, while Luigi Chinetti's New York dealership had become the channel through which Enzo Ferrari's 166 and 212 models would pass into the hands of affluent American racing and sports car enthusiasts. The success of these cars, however, was still not

Among the cleanest lines ever penned for a sports car, the rear fender, bumper, and taillight treatment of the 1956 Corvette combined all three design elements into one flowing form.

The 1957 Corvette was the first to be offered with fuel-injection. In its hottest form, the 1957 delivered 283 horsepower, one horsepower per cubic inch! A $675 option, a total of 1,040 were produced for the model year. In 1958, output was increased to 290 horsepower.

Dreams do come true. From Motorama Dream Car to Chevrolet production car was a quick step in 1953. Immediate demand for the car prompted the production of 300 Polo White cars bodied in Fiberglas. The public was so intrigued with the fiberglass concept and the fledgling plastics industry so willing to help produce the car, that Chevrolet was persuaded to continue production in fiberglass. The car pictured is an original, unrestored example.

OPPOSITE
The American ideal of a sports car had yet to be defined in the early postwar years. It took the British-built MG to open the eyes of American motorists to the joys of small, two-seat roadsters. By 1952 there were 7,449 MGs registered in the United States.

The MG's success was followed by that of the Jaguar XK120, a car that greatly influenced the design of both the 1953 Corvette and 1955 Thunderbird.

sufficient enough to convince Detroit automakers that a market for such vehicles actually existed. In 1952, a total of 11,199 new sports cars were registered in the United States. This amounted to an insignificant 0.27 percent of car registrations for the year.

Speaking before the Society of Automotive Engineers in 1953, Zora Arkus-Duntov said, "Considering the statistics, the American public does not want a sports car at all. But," he asked, "do the statistics give a true picture? As far as the American market is concerned," surmised Duntov, "it is still an unknown quantity, since an American sports car catering to American tastes, roads, way of living and national character has not yet been on the market." However, before the year was out, such a car would be on the market: the Chevrolet Corvette.

The 1953 Corvette charted new waters for GM in the realm of automotive styling, captivating a car-hungry American public that was only just beginning to understand European sports car styling.

The original Corvette body style was the closest Chevrolet ever came to creating an American sports car in the European idiom. Encompassing much of the contemporary styling seen on the Jaguar XK120, the body lines were sleek and flowing, and in true roadster form the car had no exterior door handles or roll-up side windows.

A year prior to the Corvette's introduction, one of Frank Hershey's young assistants at Ford brought him a bootlegged picture of the proposed Corvette sports car being developed at GM. Hershey and his staff, Damon Woods and L. David Ash, immediately began a crash program to develop a competitive model. "We had it roughed out in only a few weeks, and one of the guys in engineering was working on a chassis design for us," recalled Hershey.

At this time in Ford's history, the styling studio was not independent, but was under the engineering division.

Hershey reported to Earl MacPherson, then vice president in charge of engineering. "He didn't know anything about the car," says Hershey, "and what made matters worse, is that he found out about it when he caught one of his engineers working on the chassis design for me. Oh, he came storming down to my office to find out what the hell was going on. I actually think he was more angry about my having one of his engineers working on an unauthorized design than he was about my secret project. After all, we were responsible for advanced concepts, so it wasn't out of the ordinary for us to propose new models."

Hershey's staff had the exterior lines completed before Ford management ever caught wind of the project. "Now, there are a lot of stories about how the Thunderbird actually got approval," said Hershey, "about Lewis Crusoe, executive vice president of Ford, having toured the European auto shows and remarking that Ford should have a sports car like those he had seen there. He might have said that, but it wasn't what got the Thunderbird off the ground."

Of all the various stories, and there are many, Hershey actually credits Chief Production Planner Chase Morsey and Thomas B. Case, who became chief product planner on the Thunderbird project, with selling the idea to Ford management. "In fact, it was Morsey who created the personal luxury theme," recalls Hershey.

Though it is purely conjecture, Ford would likely have forestalled any sort of sports car program well into the late '50s, had Chevrolet not come out with the Corvette.

The excitement surrounding the Corvette's public debut at the 1953 New York Motorama was largely due to its sleek, futuristic appearance and unique Fiberglas body. Initially, Chevrolet planned to build only 300 Corvettes out of Fiberglas to meet dealer demands for a 1953 model and then switch to traditional steel bodies when tooling was readied. Before the final decision could be made, however, GM experienced something of an epiphany in plastic, the public was so intrigued with the concept and the fledgling plastics industry so willing to help produce the car, that Chevrolet was persuaded to continue producing the Corvette in 'glass. As it turned out, building the bodies out of plastic set GM back $400,000, whereas manufacturing them in steel would have had a tooling cost estimated at $4.5 million, so it wasn't a difficult decision.

For Ford and Hershey, it was fortunate that the Corvette came out first—it allowed them to learn from Chevrolet's mistakes! As our fickle American tastes would have it, the allure of foreign sports cars was more mystique than desire. Chevrolet had misread the signs, managing to capture the essence of the MG and Jaguar XK120 in an "Americanized" sports roadster—the kind of car people would look at, but not necessarily purchase. They wanted the styling alright, but Americans had come to expect roll-up windows, a big V-8, and choices like a hardtop or convertible, and an automatic or a manual transmission. The Corvette offered few of these amenities.

Despite its low-slung, European stance and distinction as the nation's first production car with a Fiberglas body, the Corvette's design quickly drew criticism from consumers. Following the British theory for the construction of a sports roadster, the Corvette had no exterior door handles or door locks. Presumably one would only drive with the top raised in the foulest of weather, so why put locks on a car that would have its top down most of the time? There were no roll-up windows, either. Instead, Chevrolet used removable glass side curtains.

The top itself was lightweight fabric and easily folded, innovatively stowed beneath a Fiberglas boot which added greatly to the dramatic lines of the car when the top was lowered.

All of the aforementioned features made the first Corvette immediately popular with sports car cognoscenti, those who cared not for creature comforts but more for the essence of sports car design. And that was the greatest flaw in Chevrolet's planning. Budget limitations required that Chevy engineers use an existing engine and transmission, thus the

Here is the body drop on one of the first Corvettes built in Chevrolet's St. Louis, Missouri, assembly plant in December 1953. All but the first 300 of the 250,000 Corvettes built through November 7, 1969, were built in this plant. Automobile Quarterly

One of the Corvette-based Motorama Dream cars shown in 1954 was a version fitted with a removable hardtop. The feature would not become available until 1956. Had it been introduced in 1954, Corvette sales might have been better. Chevrolet

1953 and 1954 Corvettes were powered by a moderately tweaked ohv Blue Flame six from the passenger car line, coupled to an automatic transmission. With a mere 150 horsepower and a torque converter two-speed, sports car enthusiasts who might have otherwise purchased as many cars as Chevrolet could build were anything but enthusiastic. The Corvette was intriguing to look at but less so to drive.

Ford stylist Franklin Q. Hershey, was quick to home in on the Corvette's shortcomings and when the Thunderbird came to market in the fall of 1954, it had an easily operated convertible top, plus a removable hard top, a V-8 engine, and roll-up windows. Ford called it a "Personal Luxury Car." Chevrolet called it trouble.

Official approval of Hershey's Thunderbird program didn't come from management until February 1953, exactly one year before the car's advanced preview at the Detroit Auto Show. "Time was suddenly of the essence," recalled Hershey, "and we had to have an acceptable shape within months."

Following Hershey's first design came a number of full-sized painted clay models and full scale paper drawings, each with specific variations in the body lines. Throughout the summer and fall of 1953, the Thunderbird prototypes were refined over and over, with Crusoe finally selecting the best overall design in September, the original one Hershey and his staff had done in 1952.

There were still minor elements of the Thunderbird left to be sorted out, such as exterior trim, or actually the lack of it. This became something of a personal conflict between Hershey and then design consultant George Walker (later vice president in charge of styling for Ford).

"The car was done before Walker ever got involved," says Hershey. "It was a clean, simple design that did not need accent trim." Walker, on the other hand, felt quite the opposite. While Hershey was on vacation, Walker added the new 1955 Ford Fairlane body trim to the Thunderbird. The car was photographed that way in 1954 for several ads and brochures. When Hershey returned, he had the trim removed, along with the wire wheels Walker had put on the car, and had all the photography redone, though one ad did appear in 1954 on the back cover of *Motor Trend*, showing a car with the Fairlane trim. Crusoe actually liked the Fairlane treatment but agreed with the majority that the car didn't need embellishment. His personal Thunderbird, however, had the additional trim.

As different as the Thunderbird was, it retained quite a bit of early 1950s Ford styling cues—round taillights, dual spinners on the front bumper, and as many standard parts as possible. The Thunderbird was as much disguise as development. One shining example was Ford stylist Bob Maguire's quick redo of the 1954 Astra-dial speedometer. To give the Thunderbird a dash all its own, he flanked the passenger car instrument package with a clock and tachometer and tied it all together with an engine-turned metal fascia running the width of the dashboard. Hershey commends Maguire for doing an incredible job of designing the car's interior.

As the announcement date drew near, one last element had yet to be decided—a name for the car. Ford's advertising agency, J. Walter Thompson, compiled a vast list of names, which included such gems as the Whizzette, Wombat, Monte Cristo (already being used by a sandwich), the Hawaiian, Playboy, and believe it or not, the Ford Bolero. The final list was pared down to the Apache, Beverly, Eagle, Falcon, Country Club, Tropicale, and the favorite, Savile. Notice what name wasn't on the list? It came at the 11th hour as a suggestion from Ford stylist Alden R. "Gib" Giberson. He later designed the stylized Indian Thunderbird emblem for 1956 that replaced the original Ford crest and crossed checkered flags.

Mechanically, the Thunderbird would be everything the Corvette was not. High on the list was Chevrolet's failure to give the car substantial performance. Ford answered with a new overhead valve "Y-block" V-8 engine displacing 292 cubic inches and coupled to either a manual gearbox or Ford-O-Matic automatic transmission. The four-barrel carburetor-fed 292 delivered 193 horsepower through the manual gears and 198 horsepower with the automatic.

In spite of the financial necessity to incorporate as many existing production components as possible in the Thunderbird, the one thing that had to be new was the frame. It was a convertible-type X-braced design with a 102-inch wheelbase. Front/rear track measured 56 inches, overall length was 175.2, and width measured 70.3 inches. The suspension was Ford's new independent coil spring Ball-Joint front, and leaf spring rear.

Ford had given Thunderbird buyers choices, too—the standard transmission or an overdrive

option for $110, or the Ford-O-Matic at $178 extra, either a soft convertible top, or a removable hardtop, and many of the comfort and convenience features Chevrolet's new Corvette lacked. Everyone had done their job well, from Hershey's designers, to the engineering department and marketing, through the public, which responded by purchasing 16,155 Thunderbirds the first year. Better than four times the number of Corvettes sold in 1955.

Historically, the road to progress is littered fender deep in ideas that didn't work, cars that after a few short years tumbled from lofty reverence as innovative concepts into the unclean shadows inhabited by motordom's also-rans. This was about to become the Corvette's fate. By late 1954, the car's novelty was wearing thin. The 300 built in 1953 had sold quickly but now nearly half of those produced for 1954 were languishing on dealer lots. Harley Earl's dream car was about to become a nightmare unless a Belgian-born engineer named Zora Arkus-Duntov could find a way to fix the problems that were curbing Corvette sales.

On October 14, 1954, Duntov sent a confidential memorandum to Edward N. Cole and Chevrolet engineer Maurice Olley. Wrote Duntov: "By the looks of it, the Corvette is on its way out. Dropping the car

In 1955, Chevrolet answered one demand of would-be Corvette owners with the introduction of a V-8 engine. The V-8 was a separate model listed by a different stock number and with a different base price. The V-8 displaced 265 cubic inches with a 3.75x3.0-inch bore and stroke, an 8:1 compression ratio and output of 195 horsepower. At a glance the V-8 models looked the same as six-cylinder versions but upon closer inspection those with the V-8 had an enlarged gold "V" in the name Chevrolet that appeared on the side of the car.

now will have an adverse effect internally and externally. It is admission of failure. Failure of aggressive thinking in the eyes of the organization, failure to develop a salable product in the eyes of the outside world." Duntov believed the Corvette's value had to be measured by its effect on the entire Chevrolet product line.

From the start, Duntov had been critical of the Corvette's high price, relative to its performance as a sports car. He felt that the Corvette did not offer a good value for the money. Concluded Duntov: "If the value of a car consists of practical values and emotional appeal, the sports car has very little of the first and consequently has to have an exaggerated amount of the second." In 1954, the Corvette had neither!

Ford's early success with the Thunderbird had given Chevrolet even more reasons to revive the struggling Corvette. Duntov's concerns were that Ford's aggressive advertising would exploit a Chevrolet failure and since the Corvette was an important part of changing Chevrolet's family car image, canceling the project would have been an embarrassment for both Cole and GM.

As the 1955 models were being readied for introduction, the idea of the Corvette being an embarrassment was something of a moot point, however. Chevrolet dealers were still sitting on 1,077 unsold 1954 Corvettes, amounting to nearly 30 percent of the previous year's production, and it was January 1955. For the new model year, the assembly plant in St. Louis would add only 700 new models to dealer inventory.

If nothing else, Chevrolet answered one demand of would-be Corvette owners in 1955 with the introduction of a V-8 engine, although it was really too little, too late. As was the case with the Blue Flame six, the new V-8 was also a passenger car engine that had been modified, this time equipped with a Carter four-barrel "power pack" carburetor and a special camshaft which alone accounted for 15 extra horsepower. The V-8 displaced 265 cubic inches with a 3.75x3.0 inch bore and stroke, an 8:1 compression ratio, and output of 195 horsepower. The extra horses turned the earlier Corvette's mediocre 0 to 60 time of 11 seconds inside out, dropping it to 8.7 according to *Road & Track*'s July 1955 road test. Quarter mile time improved as well falling from 18 seconds to 16.5, while top speed increased from 107.1 miles per hour to 119.1.

Despite the improvement in performance, reported *R&T*, the new low friction V-8 yielded two to three additional miles per gallon over the 150-horsepower six. After a 1,450-mile road test *Road & Track* concluded that "the V-8 gives startling performance, as might well be expected, but the transmission and brake deficiencies still will not satisfy the demands of either competitor or of the true sports car enthusiast." Test reports throughout the year showed

The styling of Ford's 1955 Thunderbird was very graceful, and like the Corvette, a grand departure from early-1950s automotive styling. Hershey and his staff, Damon Woods, and L. David Ash, actually roughed out the design in less than a month.

For three brief years Ford gave the Corvette a run for its money with a better built, more powerful, and more comfortable sports car called Thunderbird. Ford also gave buyers the options Chevrolet did not offer with the first Corvette: manual or automatic transmissions, soft convertible top or a removable hardtop, and a powerful V-8 engine.

the Corvette's brakes as "more than adequate for ordinary usage." Of course, *ordinary* was not in the sports car enthusiast's vocabulary.

More troublesome than poor brakes was the Corvette's transmission—in retrospect, a bad choice on Chevrolet's part. Though many buyers were satisfied with the two-speed Powerglide automatic gearbox neatly positioned on the floor and looking for all the world like a manual stick shift, many would have preferred more than looks. A three-speed manual was finally added as an option late in 1955. Ford had been

wise enough to see Chevrolet's error and offered both automatic and manual transmissions in 1955; one of several reasons why the early Thunderbirds were more successful.

For 1956 Ford made numerous changes in the Thunderbird but the most famous were the introductions of the porthole top and the ubiquitous Continental spare, intended to increase luggage area in the trunk, but actually de rigueur on practically everything that had wheels in the mid-1950s. Engine output was increased with an optional 312-cubic-inch V-8 devel-

With the 1956 models, output from the V-8 was increased to 210 horsepower, with 225 horsepower available through an optional dual four-barrel carburetor. The V-8 engine significantly improved the Corvette's overall weight distribution, being some 40 pounds lighter than its six-cylinder predecessor. Changes beneath the hood also demanded commensurate modifications to the suspension in order to take full advantage of the added power.

Duntov's reaction to the handling characteristics of his V-8-equipped 1955 prototype were mixed at best, and he proposed a number of engineering revisions. "The target," he explained in an *Auto Age* article, "was to attain such handling characteristics that the driver of some ability could get really high performance safely." Duntov felt this objective could be met through suspension changes that focused on "increased high-speed stability, consistent steering wheel response over a wide range of conditions and improved power transmission to the rear wheels on turns (that is, reduction of unloading of inside rear wheels)."

Several chassis modifications were made to accomplish Duntov's goal. Shims between the front crossmember and the frame increased the caster angle to two degrees. Shimming also altered the angle of the central steering idler arm so that the roll oversteer geometry was taken out of the front suspension. In concert with this, new spring hangers were used to change the slope of the rear springs thus reducing roll understeer at the rear. With these adjustments, Duntov reported, "the car goes where it is pointed and does so without hesitation. On turns taken hard, it does not plow or skid but gets into the drift. If the right amount of power is fed, the drift can be maintained without danger of the rear end getting presumptuous and assuming the position of the front." The brakes themselves were not changed, but fitted with linings that were more resistant to fade and wear.

With the V-8 and standard synchromesh three-speed manual transmission, the Corvette finally emerged as a true driver's automobile in 1956. "In almost every respect, the 1956 Corvette is a very satisfying car on the highway," wrote *Sports Cars Illustrated*, "and supplements astonishing performance with a high level of road-holding." Corvette production jumped from 700 in 1955 to a respectable 3,467 the following year.

With the introduction of the completely restyled 1956 models, Cole, Earl and Duntov had in one bold stroke redeemed the Corvette. The 1956 models were a hallmark in the evolution of the breed, the first real American sports car, cars that arrived at the momentous crossroad, and made the right turn.

At Ford, the big changes came in 1957 with a new front grille and bumper design that incorporated the bumper guards and turn indicators. The rear quarter panels received a redo by Bill Boyer, with a

As different as the Thunderbird was, it retained quite a bit of early-1950s Ford styling cues. The Thunderbird was as much disguise as development. One shining example was Ford stylist Bob Maguire's quick redo of the 1954 Astra-dial speedometer. To give the Thunderbird a dash all its own, he flanked the passenger car instrument package with a clock and tachometer and tied it all together with an engine-turned metal fascia running the width of the dashboard.

Pretty Birds in red, white and blue, well actually turquoise, display the three-year lineage of the first Thunderbird design. By the time the 1955 model had made its debut, Ford management was contemplating the two-seater's demise after the 1957 model year, an issue which eventually led to the resignation of the car's designer, Ford Chief Stylist Frank Hershey.

oping 225 horsepower. The standard 292 was boosted to 202 horsepower and also found its way into the Ford Fairlane and Crown Victoria models, which were promoted as having Thunderbird Special V-8 engines.

With planning under way for an all-new Corvette to debut in 1956, Harley Earl's team of stylists had made substantial changes to the Corvette body. Every aspect of the original design was altered and refined.

"All the designers were enamored of the Mercedes-Benz 300SL Gullwing coupe," recalled Bob Cadaret, who worked as a stylist on the Chevy design staff. "From the windshield forward, the 300SL was the predominant influence on the styling of the 1956 Corvette."

Another principal influence on the 1956 Corvette body came from the LaSalle II roadster, a 1955 GM Motorama Dream Car. The LaSalle had coved insets on the front fenders that curved well into the doors and were painted a contrasting color to accent their shape. The idea was lifted almost intact and incorporated into the design of the 1956 Corvette.

By February 1955, the basic design of the 1956 Corvette was completed. This time GM had gone to school at Ford's expense, adapting the best features of the Thunderbird. The new Corvette would have roll-up windows, with available power assist, exterior door handles, an improved convertible top mechanism, also with an available power assist, and a new extra-cost auxiliary hardtop.

design closely approximating fins, that extended from just behind the door handles to the totally restyled taillights. In keeping with the rest of the 1957 Ford line the standard engine was also updated to deliver 245 horsepower and the Thunderbird received a new dashboard.

By 1957 the Thunderbird was developing into America's number one sports car, despite Chevrolet's restyled Corvette and V-8 engines. Both were now true enthusiasts cars. To rival Chevrolet, Ford produced 208 Thunderbirds in 1957 equipped with 300-horsepower McCulloch-Supercharged engines, bettering Corvette's new 283-horsepower V-8.

The performance battle that appeared to be shaping up between Ford and Chevrolet was to be short-lived. Within Ford, two factions had been forming as the Thunderbird program progressed, and Frank Hershey found himself an almost lone defender of the car late in 1955. In January of that year, Lewis Crusoe had been promoted to executive vice president, Car and Truck Groups, and the Ford Division managership turned over to Robert S. McNamara. "He really wasn't much of a car man as I recall," said Hershey. With prompting from George Walker, McNamara decided to have the Thunderbird redesigned for 1958 as a four-passenger car.

The 1955 and 1956 Thunderbirds had been quite successful, with sales totaling over 32,000 for the first two model years. As the debate within Ford continued over the future of the two-passenger Thunderbird, Hershey suggested keeping the car and adding the four-passenger as a second model. "It wouldn't have cost anything to keep the two-seater," says Hershey, "but McNamara was determined to drop it, certain that a larger car with seating for four would increase sales." For Hershey, the die was cast. Walker had been made vice president in charge of corporate styling. He didn't want Hershey and Hershey didn't want to work for Walker. Early in 1956, and without any great fanfare, Hershey resigned from Ford. "After I left," he said, "a wave of change swept through styling." The battle within Ford was over, and the two-passenger model was laid to rest. The official line, although from whom it is not known, possibly McNamara, was "in spite of two-seaters appeal, it is not part of profit line program." Cold and short.

When word got out that the two-seater was going out of production so many orders for the 1957 model poured in that Ford had to extend the production run and the last 1957s were actually being built concurrently with the first 1958 four-seaters in order to meet demand! Bill Boyer later summed up the two-seater's demise. "As a business decision, it was well thought out. As far as Thunderbird buffs go, it was a disaster." At Chevrolet, it was probably the best news they had heard since 1955.

Design changes from 1955 through 1957 were more intricate than most people know, and it is hard to believe that the car was redesigned for 1957 with no intention of continuing production. Hershey had wanted the 1957 to continue on with the new, larger four-passenger Thunderbird as a companion model. The most notable changes from 1955 to 1957 were in the grille and bumper design and the rear fenderline, which was extended into the doors to present a starting point for the T-Bird's new tailfins.

The tail end story was a modest design change from 1955 to 1957 as the Thunderbird kept pace with Ford styling. By 1957 a trace of fin had developed.

Each of the Dream Cars gave rise to features which would appear on GM models throughout the 1950s. The front fender wells and taillight design of the Wildcat II found their way into the Buick Skylark. The Bonneville's contributions, aside from the name used by Pontiac on its all-new 1957 sport models, were the dual Silver Streaks over the hood, used on 1955 models.

Of the three, the Olds F-88 was closest to a production car and could have made the step from Dream Car to road car as easily as the Corvette, had Oldsmobile decided to enter the emerging sports car market of the 1950s.

Oddly enough, though, the F-88 had little impact on Olds styling; mainly because Oldsmobile introduced its 1955 models a full year ahead of schedule on January 20, 1954, in an effort to keep pace with new designs from Ford and Chrysler.

Closest to the Corvette in styling, the F-88 could have been produced at the St. Louis, Missouri, assembly plant alongside the Chevrolets, had GM wanted a companion car to the Corvette, but with an unsold inventory of 1954 Corvettes still on dealer lots it was hard enough for one GM division to field such a radical concept. Why then did Buick, Pontiac, and Oldsmobile tempt the

It has been said that the only difference between a dream and reality is in the doing. No statement could better describe the GM Motorama cars built in the 1950s. Throughout the era, the General Motors Art & Colour Section, Chief Stylist Harley Earl, and his talented staff of designers kept Americans spellbound with futuristic concepts, many of which found their way into production, either in part, or entirely—such as the 1953 Chevrolet Corvette.

It was Earl's uncanny ability to gauge and determine new directions in automotive styles that kept the Motorama cars continually intriguing, and more often than not, what Earl proposed in his Dream Cars was not too far from reality.

When the Corvette made its public debut in 1953, a trio of similar cars was waiting in the wings for the 1954 Motorama, all of like design to the Corvette, but each distinctively tailored to their respective GM divisions; the Buick Wildcat II, Pontiac Bonneville Special and Oldsmobile F-88. All three had Fiberglas bodies, and shared the Corvette's basic platform design, wraparound windshield and fundamental styling proportions.

In 1958, Ford abandoned the original Thunderbird sports car concept replacing it with a new unibody-construction four-passenger car. The new Thunderbirds were built on the same line as the Continental Mk III. The new model left the field wide open for Chevrolet which welcomed the demise of Hershey's sales-stealing two-seater. Ironically, Ford General Manager Robert S. McNamara had been correct in his evaluation of the market. The four-passenger Thunderbird was far more successful. However, to sports car enthusiasts, the T-Bird was dead.

public with cars they had no intention of building? To answer that question, you have to look beyond the obvious. The GM marketing departments were not responsible for creating Dream Cars, it was the Advanced Styling Sections, and each GM division had their own semi-autonomous studio operated under the watchful eye of Art & Colour chief Harley Earl. "It was their job to stretch the envelope," says retired General Motors Director of Design Dave Holls.

There were many influences in the design of the 1956 Corvette. One of the most interesting was the 1954 Mercedes-Benz 300SL. Recalled Bob Cadaret, who worked as a stylist on the Chevy design staff, "All the designers were enamored of the Mercedes-Benz 300SL Gullwing coupe." From the windshield forward, the 300SL was the dominant influence on the styling of the 1956 Corvette. The most dramatic design element of the 1956 Corvette was the fender cove which curved back into the door. The principal influence for this design was the LaSalle II roadster, a 1955 GM Motorama Dream Car. The idea was lifted almost intact and incorporated into the 1956 Corvette.

Ironically, had the F-88 been given approval, it would have been a far superior car to the Corvette, as it would have been powered by Olds' Rocket V-8, instead of Chevy's underpowered Blue Flame six. Had Olds produced the F-88, it would have been a rakish, low-slung open two-seater from the same school of design as the Jaguar XK-120, Kaiser-Darrin, and Nash-Healey—all of which had been influential in GM's styling of the Corvette.

Holls, who was a freshman designer under Harley Earl in the 1950s, said that the Pontiac, Olds and Buick versions were never considered for production. "You have to understand, that [in 1953] little was 'in,' and the idea of a personalized sports car was foremost on Harley Earl's mind." Building the F-88 would have been duck soup after the Corvette. Earl wanted to see some expressions of beautiful smaller cars done throughout the divisions, but the Olds and the others were never going to happen because the Corvette was already there. The corporation didn't want anything competitive."

Although quite similar to the Corvette, the F-88 had a number of innovative features that would have been quite interesting in a sports car of the 1950s. Foremost was the interior design. Instrumentation was "competition-type": rather than being mounted across the dashboard in conventional style, the speedometer, temperature, fuel gauge and clock started at the center of the dash panel, extended vertically to the floor and then were placed along the transmission tunnel, dividing the seat compartment. This gave the driver an uninterrupted view of the road over the dashboard. The radio was console mounted as well, with controls for tuning and volume flanking a round station selector dial.

What the 1953 through 1955 Corvettes lacked, the 1956 Corvette more than made up. Like the 1955 Thunderbird, the new Corvette offered roll-up windows, with available power assist, exterior door handles, an improved convertible top mechanism, also with an available power assist, and a new extra-cost auxiliary hardtop.

The car had no interior door handles. Instead, you simply pressed a button on the upper center of the door to release the latch. A push-button was also used on the exterior for opening the door. Lavishly upholstered, the interior and steering wheel were finished in pigskin.

From the exterior, the F-88 was distinctively Oldsmobile with a large oval honeycomb grille, and an Olds emblem on the hood. Power came from an advanced version of the Rocket 88 engine, displacing 324 cubic inches and developing 250 horsepower.

One of the car's unique features was the spare tire compartment, mounted horizontally behind the rear bumper. The center section of the integral bumper guard was designed to drop down, revealing a spare tire conveniently mounted on rollers to facilitate easy removal.

The exhaust system was another clever feature. Rather than being routed under the body or through

With the 1956 models, output from the V-8 was increased to 210 horsepower, with 225 horsepower available through an optional dual four-barrel carburetor.

Jim Jeffords racing the Purple People Eater Mk III at Riverside in July 1959. Bob Tronolone

the bumpers, it exited through the lower rear fenders in oval openings, accented by decorative louvers just ahead of the ports on the fender panel.

Continuing the aircraft theme created by the grille and instrument design, the wheel covers were jet airfoil disks that gave a turbine effect. Built on a Corvette-based 102-inch chassis, the car's overall length was 167 inches, with a windshield height of just 48 inches.

There was nothing really radical about the two F-88s built for 1954's Motorama, explained Holls, except to the public. "It was an era of Dream Cars and it was wonderful. Everybody loved the Motorama and we were beating the pants off Ford and Chrysler with show cars."

After the Motorama season, said Holls, the cars were supposed to be destroyed. "There had been a terrible problem with the 1953s, because they were all running cars and got into the hands of people outside of the corporation. It was nothing but a disaster," remembered Holls. "They were thrown together for a show and were not really roadworthy. People wanted the cars and GM didn't really think that much about it, so they sold them. Afterward though, they were impossible to keep running or repair. Even the paint was impossible to match if you got a chip. Everything was custom built, so there were no [spare] parts. After that, GM said that all of the Motorama cars were to be scrapped in 1954 and 1955. A lot of them were actually saved at GM, but none were sold," says Holls. "A

lot of us lamented the loss of the cars that were scrapped, but the attitude at GM was that 'you shouldn't whine about it. Don't live in the past.' So you kind of kept your mouth shut, went on and did new cars."

Throughout the early 1950s, Ford and Chevrolet had never been completely alone. There was competition, but it was of little consequence to Detroit's giants. To sports car enthusiasts, however, names like Crosley, Nash-Healey, Kaiser-Darrin, Kurtis, and Devin meant as much or more than Corvette and Thunderbird.

Of the lot, the innovative Kaiser-Darrin was the most interesting and the closest to the Corvette as it also wore a body manufactured out of Fiberglas. As the name implied, the car was designed by the renowned automotive stylist Howard "Dutch" Darrin, who had to his credit some of the most spectacular Duesenberg designs of the 1930s, the 1939 Packard Hollywood Darrin and 1942 Packard Clipper. Henry J. Kaiser, who had decided to challenge the Detroit establishment in 1946 by starting his own automotive company, along with partner Joseph Frazer, the former president of Willys-Overland and then Graham-Paige, hired Darrin to create the two-seat sports car shortly after the Corvette made its debut. The company's ephemeral success lasted just nine years but ended on a Darrin scored note with the innovative Fiberglas sports car introduced in 1954.

The rakish, low-slung, 1954 Olds F-88 sports car was as close to a production prototype as any GM Dream Car since the 1953 Chevrolet Corvette. Had there been more enthusiasm at Oldsmobile, says former GM Design Director Dave Holls, the F-88 could have been built.

Production began at Kaiser's Jackson, Michigan, warehouse and then was transferred to Toledo, Ohio. Although Kaiser discontinued the car after only 435 were built, Darrin purchased 50 bodies and chassis, and fitted them with Cadillac engines (similar to the hybrid Cadillac-powered Allard race cars of the '50s), and sold them from his Los Angeles shop. The last Darrin built was sold in 1958. Kaiser had announced the end of automobile production three years before. After a promising start in 1946 and 1947, Kaiser and company had posted losses through 1955 totaling $92 million. Even the great Henry J. Kaiser couldn't beat Detroit at its own game.

Radio manufacturing pioneer Powell Crosley also wanted to get in the automotive game, and he thought he could run with the big boys by going after a segment of the automotive market Detroit hadn't even considered.

The tiny Crosley auto, originally powered by a 580-cc twin-cylinder engine was first introduced in 1939. After the war, Crosley production started up in Marion, Indiana, using a 721-cc "COBRA" (for COpper BRAzed) four-cylinder engine originally developed for the Navy. The block of this engine was made

Olds F-88 instrumentation was the "competition-type," resembling aircraft instruments. Rather than being located across the dashboard in conventional style, the instruments started at the center of the dash panel, extended vertically to the floor, and then were placed along the transmission tunnel, dividing the seat compartment. The radio was console-mounted as well with controls for tuning and volume flanking a round dial.

The F-88 was powered by a 250-horsepower advanced version of the "Rocket" engine. Displacement was 324 cubic inches

The fiberglass-bodied Kaiser-Darrin was designed for Henry J. Kaiser by renowned automotive stylist Howard "Dutch" Darrin. Although Kaiser discontinued the car after only 435 were built, Darrin purchased 50 bodies and chassis, fitted them with Cadillac engines and continued to sell them from his Los Angeles shop until 1958.

Radio pioneer Powell Crosley took his best shot at the emerging U.S. sports car market in 1950 when he introduced the Hotshot. Powered by a 26.7-horsepower, 750 cc CIBA engine, the tiny two-passenger Hotshot out-performed anything in its class and became a popular club racer in the 1950s.
Automobile Quarterly

LEFT AND OPPOSITE
Bill Devin's SS was one of the most exciting limited-production sports cars of the 1950s. The car used a substantial tubular frame, 283-cubic-inch, 290-horsepower Chevrolet engine and Italian-inspired bodywork fabricated from fiberglass. A fully equipped Devin SS sold for $5,950. Only 15 or so were produced, although Devin had originally intended to build 150 to gain approval for SCCA racing.
Automobile Quarterly

The Kurtis sports car was no pretender. On August 27, 1949, at Bonneville Salt Flats, a standard Kurtis model, with Wally Parks at the wheel, averaged 142.515 miles per hour for a measured mile. The engine used for this run was a Ford V-8 with full Edelbrock equipment. Frank Kurtis is shown below with an early Kurtis sports car. Dr. Paul Sable collection

of oven-brazed copper and sheet steel with a fixed cylinder head. Unfortunately, this design was prone to failure, and in 1949, it was succeeded by a new cast-iron-block-assembly (CIBA) engine. The 1949, Crosley predated Nash's tiny Metropolitan as one of the smallest cars ever produced in the United States.

In 1949, Crosley also introduced one of this country's first postwar sports cars, the Hotshot. The tiny, two-passenger Hotshot shared the same single-overhead-cam, five main-bearing, 750-cc, CIBA four-cylinder engine as the rest of the Crosley line and was the first production automobile to be fitted with disc brakes.

The tiny two-passenger Hotshot out-performed anything in its class and became a popular club racer in the 1950s. With an engine output of 26.5 horsepower at 5,400 rpm and a very forgiving suspension, the lightweight Crosley had the ability to make a mediocre driver look formidable.

The Hotshot had an impressive performance-per-dollar ratio unheard of up to that time. Ninety miles per hour was possible right out of the box, and

The Kurtis sports car was essentially a parts bin creation with 95 percent of its critical components available at nearby parts counters. The 100-inch wheelbase chassis carried an aluminum body with steel doors and fiberglass hood and rear deck. Kurtis production ended after only 36 of his 1950 models had been built. The design was sold to wealthy TV and radio manufacturer Earl "Mad Man" Muntz. The new Muntz Car Company produced the Kurtis Sports Cars on a longer wheelbase, making them four-seaters, but with the same basic body lines. Muntz used Cadillac V-8 engines and produced 28 examples in 1950. In 1951, Muntz lengthened the wheelbase again and produced the bodies in steel rather than aluminum and offered a removable hardtop. Power was supplied by a Lincoln V-8. In 1951 and 1952, Muntz sold 230 cars. For 1953 and 1954 Muntz sold another 136 cars before turning the company back to Frank Kurtis in 1954.
Automobile Quarterly

its excellent handling allowed an example to capture the 1951 Index of Performance at the 12 Hours of Sebring. A number of SCCA novices launched their competition careers by supplying stern views of their Class H Crosleys to otherwise adequate drivers mounted in Class F MG TCs, TDs, and Singers.

Unfortunately, none of Powell Crosley's cars were popular enough to keep him in business. In 1952, Crosley joined the ranks of would-be automakers whose sales had plummeted in the postwar 1950s. Crosley had filled the pipeline and there were too few buyers left. From a record high of 24,871 cars in 1948, sales had fallen to just 1,522 cars in 1952.

Another obscure but no less admirable sports car was the Devin SS. Designer Bill Devin and partner Ernie McAfee had life by the tail in the early 1950s when they peddled exotic Italian sports cars to rich playboys in Southern California. One of the cars was an attractive Ermini 1100 that Bill had sold to Jim Orr, but not before he had lifted a fiberglass mold from the Ermini's exquisite Scaglietti open two-seater coachwork. From this first mold he created scaled-up modular versions that would accommodate any chassis/driveline combination.

In 1958, Devin filled an order for a body to match a one-off chassis, independent front and De Dion rear with inboard disc brakes aft, and a 283-cubic-inch Corvette powertrain. Christened "Devin SS," 0 to 60 arrived in under 5 seconds and 0 to 100 miles per hour in 12 seconds. Flat out top speed was an unnerving 140 miles per hour.

From 1958 to 1961, only 15 were produced but they gained such fame that today a Devin SS body decorates the entrance to the Rosso-Bianco Automobile Collection at Aschaffenburg (not far from Frankfurt).

Frank Kurtis was another legendary 1950s-era sports car builder, only unlike many of his contemporaries, Kurtis' name was already well known. From 1928 to 1948, he had built an enviable reputation for racing car design, producing everything from Midgets to Indy cars. In 1949, when Johnny Parsons qualified the prototype Kurtis-Kraft 3000 at Indianapolis, setting a record (for unblown cars) of 132.9 miles per hour, he raised the curtain on what became known as the "Frank Kurtis Era" at that venue. It could be said that Kurtis reached his Indy apogee in 1953 when 23 of the 36 starters were sitting in Kurtis-Kraft cars.

One of Frank's more endearing contributions to the sports-racing milieu was the Kurtis sports car. With 95 percent of its critical components available at nearby parts counters, it arrived with a 100-inch wheelbase, 68-inch width, 169-inch overall length, and a weight of only 2,300 pounds. The body was aluminum with steel doors and a fiberglass hood and rear deck.

A variety of engines was available, including the

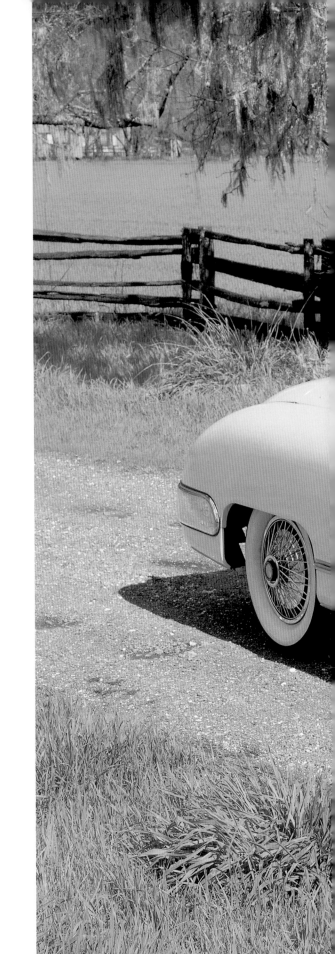

new 160-horsepower Cadillac V-8, but the limited capacity of Kurtis' factory prevented production of more than 30 cars.

What few people realize today is that long before the Corvette, Thunderbird or even Kaiser-Darrin, America had a terrific sports car, the 1951 Nash Healey. The short-lived two-seater was another hybrid, combining the efforts of George Mason, president of Nash, British sports car maker Donald Healey, and renowned Italian designer Battista "Pinin" Farina.

Mason already had a working relationship with Pinin Farina who had also designed the 1952 Nash. From 1952 to 1954 Pinin Farina built the sporty bodies in Italy and mounted them on chassis supplied by Healey and powered by specially tuned Nash Ambassador six-cylinder engines. The earlier 1951 models had been built in England with a body by Healey. A total of 504 Nash Healeys were produced between December 1950 and August 1954. Priced at $6,000, it was one of the most expensive automobiles sold in the United States at the time. It was also one of the most attractive sports cars of the 1950s, or any era for that matter.

The 1950s saw the emergence of the sports car as an American ideal. While most automakers failed to create a valid sports car that could sell in great enough numbers to be profitable (or those who could, couldn't build them), the seeds had been sewn. Out of the 1950s came a demand from American automotive enthusiasts for newer and more practical sports cars. The Mustang, Camaro, Firebird, AMX, and others that followed in the 1960s owe their existence to the Devins, Kaiser-Darrins, Crosleys, Corvettes, and two-seat Thunderbirds that preceded them.

Lew Florence powers his Chrysler-powered Kurtis through turn 6 at Laguna Seca during a Cal Club regional race in 1958. Bob Tronolone

The 1951 Nash Healey combined the talents of George Mason, president of Nash, British sports car maker Donald Healey, and renowned Italian designer Battista "Pinin" Farina. Nash supplied specially tuned Ambassador six-cylinder engines to Healey, which were mounted to a Healey-built chassis and then shipped to Italy where Pinin Farina built the bodies. The cost of the multinational sports car was a staggering $6,000. In 1951, the most expensive American-made car, the Cadillac Fleetwood Seventy-Five, cost only $5,098. Nash sold a total of 504 Nash Healeys between December 1950 and August 1954. Automobile Quarterly

CHAPTER 8

REBORN TO BE WILD

Hot Rods and Customs of the 1950s

The late Dean Batchelor once defined a hot rod as "any production car which has been modified to provide more performance." A pretty broad definition, but Dean was rather broad minded when it came to automobiles. He loved everything from dry lake dragsters to Duesenbergs. His last book, *The American Hot Rod,* was a tribute to his favorite subject. Before he became an expert on classic cars and Ferraris, before he ever edited a magazine or became Editorial Director of *Road & Track,* Dean was a hot rodder.

During the years I served as associate publisher of *Rod Action* magazine, Dean and I had countless discussions about the content of the magazine which was continually expanding from its purist rodding roots to include customs, which at the time I did not believe belonged in *Rod Action.* It was Dean who enlightened me (as he had so many times before) about his broad interpretation of hot rods. The name itself, as Dean explained in his book, came about in 1945. Hot rods, at least in the context of hot rods as we recognize them today, really didn't come into their own until the postwar 1950s, but that doesn't mean they didn't exist.

In the late 1940s and early 1950s, Dean was among a handful of rodders who raced on the dry lake beds at Rosamond and El Mirage in the California desert and at the Bonneville Salt Flats in Utah. Dean managed to race just about everything from his 1932 Ford roadster to the 193mph *So-Cal Special* streamliner, which he drove at Bonneville. Along with partner Alex Xydias, Dean was one of hot rodding's pioneers. Behind him, however, was a generation of teens who were just beginning to find out what Batchelor and his friends already knew: Hot rods were more than cars—they were a lifestyle.

In the 1950s, the hot rod became the essence of manhood for thousands of teenagers. They were cheap, easy to build (assuming you had basic mechanical skills), and nothing turned a young girl's head faster than a candy apple red deuce coupe with a rumbling V-8 under its hood.

The Ford V-8 in this 1932 was long gone when it became a hot rod in 1951. The Ford motor was replaced with a high-compression Oldsmobile engine fitted with over-the-counter speed equipment and Edelbrock manifold.

The typical 1950s era hot rod, this 1932 hi-boy roadster is a mixture of cars and parts—a 1932 Ford frame, 1929 body, and a custom hood. This all original roadster was built in 1951.

Hot rod interiors were pretty simple in the 1950s, especially in the case of home-builts where everything came from either the scrap yard or from a local speed shop. Note the dash decal from Speed Specialties in Pacific Palisades, California.

Hot rods may have come into their own in the 1950s, but the idea was anything but new. In the 1920s, they were known simply as "hopped up" cars and models like this 1924 Ford Model T fitted with a Fronty engine and Speedster body by Mercury were typical of prewar hot rods. The styling of the car, absent of fenders and with a short rear deck inspired the look of cars built by rodders in the early postwar era.

Southern California had always been on the cutting edge of style, even as far back as the 1920s when Harley Earl was an independent auto stylist in Los Angeles and the Walter M. Murphy Company in Pasadena was recognized as one of the leading coachbuilders in the world. More than half a century later, Southern California is still a Mecca for automotive trends. Almost every major automaker has a styling or research and development studio in California. It should come as no surprise then, that hot rodding is deeply rooted in Southern California. Whether it started there, or on the East Coast, will be debated forever.

Batchelor's theory was that hot rodding developed in Southern California and grew faster there than it did elsewhere. "My own perception," wrote Dean in *The American Hot Rod*, "has been that the modifications of production engines started at about the same time in the Northeast, Midwest, and West— the difference being that those engines built in the East and Midwest went into sprint cars to be raced on oval tracks, while the engines built up in the West typically went into street cars."

While hot rods may not have come into their own until the 1950s, the theory of hot rod design itself

Renowned hot rodder, convertible top builder, and upholsterer Tony Nancy built this car in 1957. Number 22Jr was a highly modified 1929 Model A body mounted on a 1932 Ford frame. Designed as a dragster, the car was powered by a blown 256-cubic-inch flathead Ford.

Photographed in the late 1950s, this picture shows Tony Nancy's blown Model A in action. A drag strip car, this one never ran on the dry lakes. Running in the X-Fuel Roadster Class, Tony held both the ET and Top Speed class records, the latter at 136.42 miles per hour. Greg Sharp, NHRA Historical Services

is almost as old as the automobile. Back in 1924, you could take an old Model T Ford, rebuild the engine, throw away the body and fit the chassis with any one of a half dozen speedster bodies on the market from Maxwell (not the Maxwell car company), Laurel, Bud, Fordspeed, Ames, Paco, and Mercury. The Mercury speedster, produced by the Mercury Body Corporation of Louisville, Kentucky, was an almost exact depiction of what a hot rod would look like some 25 years later, and for the 1920s, this "hopped up" Model T was exactly that, a primordial hot rod.

To increase horsepower, the Ford flathead four beneath the hood was usually fitted with Fronty heads, designed by Louis and Arthur Chevrolet. Probably the first instance of a "Chevy" engine going into a Ford. The most popular engine modifications to the Model T were manufactured by Frontenac and Rajo. The Fronty Ford engines, however, were no lightweights, as handily demonstrated in 1923 when a dohc, 16-valve Fronty-powered racer finished fifth in the Indianapolis 500 Mile Race.

In the 1920s, adventurous young drivers were racing modified coupes and roadsters across dry lake beds in California's high desert, at Rosamond, Harper, and Muroc Dry Lakes. By the 1930s high-performance roadsters and early streamliners were testing their limits from the Mojave desert to Daytona Beach, Florida.

Not only did the design of salt flats racers inspire the hot rods of the 1950s, many of those young racers from the 1930s became the car builders and engine tuners of the 1950s. They were the creators of the modern-day speed shop.

If any automobile lent itself to being "hopped up" it was the 1932 Ford. They were plentiful and cheap. "If you were a 'hot rodder' in the years

ABOVE AND FAR LEFT
The simplicity of the traditional 1932 Ford hot rod has been a standard in the hobby for over 40 years. This 1932 Ford roadster, known as the Checker Car, *was originally built in the 1970s, though it's based on 1950s styling. Like many Ford hot rods, this one ended up with a GM engine under the hood, in this instance a 450-horsepower Chevy V-8. The styling of the* Checker Car *is the ideal of a 1950s era hot rod.*

Considered to be the quintessential street rod of the 1950s, The Outlaw *was built by Ed "Big Daddy" Roth in 1959. This was one of the first custom rods not based on a production car, fitted instead with a totally fabricated fiberglass body. Roth used Ford running gear under his one-of-a-kind design.* The Outlaw *was Roth's first custom automobile and the inspiration for legions of copies. This car helped thrust Roth to the forefront of the mod rod movement in the 1960s.*

that found their way into tract home garages where teens, with a little help from their fathers and friends, renovated tread bare and road worn models. A junkyard Model T, Model A, or 1932 Ford could be found for as little as $25. You scrounged around for parts in salvage yards, old garages, just about anywhere imaginable. A chassis from one car, the engine and transmission from another and a pieced-together body.

Hot rods became an art form, automotive sculpture created with lead, blow torches and imagination. Chopped, channeled, mixed, and matched. The idea wasn't to restore an old car but to create something new. A roadster or coupe that was lighter and faster than it had originally been.

There seemed to be only one rule when it came to building a hot rod: change everything. Increase engine displacement, throw on dual quads, add a blower, junk the old flathead, and drop in a Cadillac V-8—whatever it took to get more horsepower, more speed, and make a car that was faster than the next guy's. And hopefully "the next guy" wasn't a young Gene Winfield or Mickey Thompson!

Winfield, who still designs and builds hot rods and customs in his Southern California shop in Canoga Park, started out in 1946 building cars to run on the dry lakes. "When I opened my first shop I specialized in porting and relieving flathead blocks, I was dropping my own axles, making steering plates, pretty much all hot rod stuff. I opened a bigger shop in Modesto in 1953, and by then the customs were becoming popular. Little by little I got into custom body work.

"It wasn't so much a lack of enthusiasm for what Detroit was building in the 1950s that generated inter-

between 1940 and 1955," wrote Batchelor, "the chances are you wanted a 1932 roadster. In the immediate post-WWII years hot-rodded 1932 Fords were everywhere." Even to this day, the 1932 Ford is the foundation of street rodding, the car most commonly modified or reproduced in fiberglass.

Hot rods of the 1950s were almost all junk cars in the beginning, high school auto shop projects est in hot rods," said Winfield. "People wanted something different, a hot rod or street rod type that looked cool. By the early 1950s I was doing almost all straight body work and customs. Back then we were chopping tops, frenching headlights and taillights, and that's where I got my reputation as a customizer."

Winfield was a contemporary of Batchelor and Xydias and had already established himself as a racer, winning more than 50 drag racing trophies. "The first time I ever ran the dry lakes I went to see Alex Xydias and Doane Spencer, who was working for him as a fabricator and mechanic, and they told me how to set up my car to run El Mirage. With my 248-cubic-inch flathead engine, gear ratios, cam, and everything, I asked them how fast I should expect to go and they said 120 miles per hour. I was in the Century Toppers Auto Club so I had to make sure I would break 100 miles per hour but that seemed like a lot. Sure enough they were right. I clocked 112 miles per hour my first time out and on the second run 121 miles per hour. I got my first trophy in Reno shortly after in June 1949.

"It was mostly younger people back then, very few older guys were into hot rods unlike today. Of course, that was my generation. Today we are the older guys!"

The American hot rod was in its hey day during the 1950s. A typical weekend at El Mirage saw hundreds of spectators and nearly as many cars. Greg Sharp NHRA Historical Services

The biggest name in customs was George Barris. This 1940 Mercury was one of his earlier cars and features unique blue window glass.

The interior of a typical 1950s custom was either vinyl or leather tuck and roll. While plenty of customizers specialized in upholstery, in Southern California it was common practice to take the car across the border to Tiajuana, Mexico, where there were dozens of upholstery shops that specialized in cheap but well done tuck and roll. Acrylic knobs were another popular interior touch used by customizers in the 1950s.

By the early 1950s, just building a hot rod wasn't enough. For car builders like George Barris, Harry Westergard, or Dean Moon, the idea was to create a car so distinctive in appearance that it became a work of art, the automotive equivalent of expressionism. Customs became the canvas upon which imaginative customizers like Barris and Winfield would paint a new portrait of the American automobile. Cars that had already lived one life were about to be reborn.

"From 1953 on I was doing almost all custom work," recalls Winfield. "We were working on Oldsmobiles, Chevys, and Mercurys. I think Mercurys were the most popular by a wide margin. That's one thing we've talked about around here off and on for several years now. How come all the 1949, 1950, and 1951 Mercs keep showing up? An incredible number of Mercs have been saved over the years in comparison to other cars from the same era. That body style

was so perfect for customizing. Those cars have been around now for thirty, forty years."

By the mid-1950s, hot rods had begun to die down and customs really dominated. "That trend reversed itself a decade later," says Winfield, "when Detroit started building muscle cars. The late 1950s really marked the heyday of the custom."

Hot rods not only brought forth a new generation of automotive enthusiasts but a new way of expressing that enthusiasm—the "stoplight grand prix." Street racing. By the mid-1950s, Hollywood was cranking out teen hot rod movies by the dozens, *Devil on Wheels*, *Hot Rod Girl*, *Teenage Thunder*, *High School Caesar*, and at least one classic, *Rebel Without A Cause*. Every one of them involved hot rods and road races. Hollywood was beginning to paint a picture of hot rod owners as bad boys. And some were.

While drag racing on city streets was overplayed by the movie industry, it wasn't too far from the truth. Fortunately, there was another way for young men to prove their mechanical and driving skills besides tearing down Main Street after school or racing over back roads at night. It was sanctioned drag racing, in the form of the National Hot Rod Association (NHRA), which was founded by *Hot Rod* magazine editor Wally Parks in 1951. Parks and the NHRA gave everyone with a hot rod a chance to show what it could do.

On the flip side from organized drag racing, speed record challengers, and high-buck customs, were the average Joes, shade-tree mechanics, high school and college students, and blue collar workers with a passion for speed and a penchant for old Fords, Chevys, and Mercs. They spent their evenings and weekends in the garage, building cars that reflected their tastes and talents, and what inspired them most

By the early 1950s just building a hot rod wasn't enough. For guys like George Barris, Harry Westergard, or Dean Moon, the idea was to create a car so distinctive in appearance that it became a work of art. Customs became the automotive equivalent of expressionism. Far from the traditional hot rod, customs were built out of late 1940s and early 1950s cars. Next to Fords, Mercurys were among the most popular cars for customizing. This 1950 Mercury coupe was customized by Joe Bailon in the mid-1950s.

To give the 1950 Merc more character, Bailon chopped the top, slanted the B pillars, and smoothed out the belt line to give it a longer, lower shape. The 1950 Mercury lent itself to being customized and there are probably more chopped Mercs than any other car from the 1950s. Bailon originally painted the car Candy Apple Red, a color that he invented. In the late 1960s, the Merc was refurbished and painted in black nitrocellulose lacquer.

usually came from the pages of *Hot Rod* magazine and *Rod & Custom*, back in the days when *R&C* was small enough to fold up and stuff in your back pocket.

Typical of 1950s-era hot rods are the cars pictured in this chapter. The 1932 Hi-Boy Roadster pictured in front of a drive-in restaurant, is a mixture of cars and parts, including a 1932 Ford frame, 1929 body, and a custom hood. The conversion took place in 1951 when the Ford motor was replaced with a high-compression Oldsmobile engine fitted with over-the-counter speed equipment. The ohv Olds engine was a logical choice because it offered more power than most Ford flatheads could muster.

Number 22Jr, built by the legendary Tony Nancy in 1957, was a heavily modified 1929 Model A Ford roadster body mounted on a 1932 Ford frame. Designed as a dragster, the car was so radical for its time that it ended up on the December 1957 cover of *Hot Rod*. The blown 256-cubic-inch flathead Ford propelled the car to a 10.4-second quarter mile and a top speed of 137 miles per hour.

The *Checker Car*, named for its distinctive paint scheme, is owned by noted car collector Bruce Meyer, and began life as a 1932 Ford roadster. It was originally built in the 1970s and became a top 10 winner in National Street Rod Association (NSRA) competition. Later it was redone by Pete Chapouris, of Pete & Jake's and *California Kid* fame. Like many Ford hot rods, this one ended up with a GM engine under the hood, in this instance a 450-horsepower Chevy V-8. The styling of the *Checker Car* is the ideal of a 1950s-era hot rod.

The Outlaw, owned today by Bruce Lustman, is considered to be the quintessential "street rod" of the 1950s, built by Ed "Big Daddy" Roth in 1959. *The Outlaw* was one of the first custom rods not based on a production car, fitted instead with a totally fabricated body. While Ford running gear was used to power the car, Roth built the body out of fiberglass, making it a one-of-a-kind design. *The Outlaw* was Roth's first custom automobile and the inspiration for legions of copies. This car helped thrust Roth to the forefront of the mod rod movement in the 1960s.

The red 1940 Mercury convertible was done by Hollywood customizer George Barris, whose signature touch on this car was the use of blue glass for the windows. One of Barris' earliest creations, the car has been restored over the years by several owners, who always preserved the Barris styling and that rare blue glass.

Next to Fords, Mercurys were among the most popular cars for customizing. The 1950 Mercury coupe, owned today by Bruce Meyer, was customized by Joe Bailon. The inventor of Candy Apple Red paint color, Bailon did the Merc in the mid-1950s. To give the car more character, Bailon chopped the top, slanted the B pillars, and smoothed out the belt line to give it a longer, lower shape. "A lot of lead work must have gone into this car," said Meyer. "The Mercury

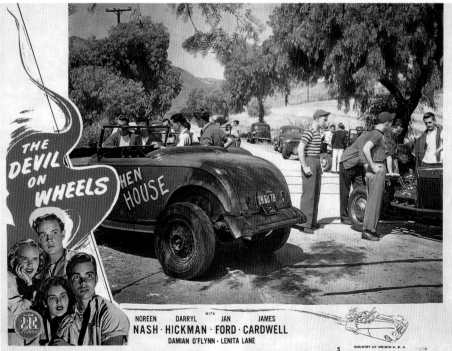

was the car of choice for the chop guys back in the 1950s. It just sort of lent itself to being customized. There are probably more chopped Mercs than any other cars." Originally painted Candy Apple Red, in the late 1960s it was redone in black nitrocellulose lacquer, which has lasted for over 30 years.

They may have torn down the Tiny Naylors, Du Pars, and Sonic drive-in restaurants of the 1950s, and Detroit has certainly given up on the individuality of models that so clearly defined cars of the 1950s, but hot rods and customs seem to have prevailed. When the year 2000 comes around you won't find Detroit automakers turning out 1959 Eldorados again, but you might still come across a brand-new 1932 Ford Hi-Boy.

Of all the cars that we associate with the 1950s, the hot rod is the only one that has survived the test of time and it may well become the most nostalgic automobile of the 20th century. The last best piece of an era we remember as The Fifties.

Index

RECOMMENDED READING

Adler, Dennis. Corvettes—The Cars that Created the Legend. Iola, Wisconsin: Krause Publications, 1996.

Batchelor, Dean. The American Hot Rod. Osceola, Wisconsin: Motorbooks International, 1995.

Dammann, George H., 70 Years of Chrysler. Sarasota, Florida: Crestline Publishing, 1974.

Dammann, George H. and James K. Wagner. The Cars of Lincoln Mercury. Sarasota, Florida: Crestline Publishing, 1987.

Halberstam, David. The Fifties. New York: Villard Books, 1993.

Langworth, Richard M. Personal Luxury—The Thunderbird Story. Osceola, Wisconsin: Motorbooks International, 1980.

Ludvigsen, Karl. Corvette, America's Star-Spangled Sports Car. 2nd Ed. Princeton, New Jersey: Princeton Publishing, Inc., 1978.

McCall, Walter M.P. 80 Years of Cadillac LaSalle. Sarasota, Florida: Crestline Publishing, 1982.

Mueller, Mike. Fifties American Cars. Osceola, Wisconsin: Motorbooks International, 1994.